Christopher Hitchens

letters to a
young contrarian

BASIC

BOOKS

A Member of the Perseus Books Group

Published by Basic Books,
A Member of the Perseus Books Group

Designed by Rick Pracher

Library of Congress Cataloging-in-Publication Data
Hitchens, Christopher.
   Letters to a young contrarian / Christopher Hitchens.
   p.   cm.
   ISBN 0–465–03032–7
   1. Conformity. 2. Dissenters. 3. Radicalism.   I. Title.
HM1246 .H57 2001
303.3'2--dc21   2001035273

03   04/ 10   9   8   7   6   5   4

In memory of Peter Sedgwick

My dear X,

Now that it's time to launch this little paper boat onto the tide, I thought I would write you a closing letter by way of beginning. While the book has been with its editors and printers, I have been occupied on several other fronts, as you know. And a stray question of yours floated into my mind: How do I respond when I see myself or my efforts abused or misrepresented in the public prints?

The brief answer is that I have become inured without becoming indifferent. I attack and criticise people myself; I have no right to expect lenience in return. And I don't believe those authors who say that they don't care about reviews or notices. However, it does tire me to read, time and again, reviews and notices that are based on clippings from earlier reviews and notices. Thus, there's always an early paragraph, usually written in a standard form of borrowed words, that says "Hitchens, whose previous targets have even included Mother Teresa and Princess Diana as well as Bill Clinton, now turns to . . . ."

Of course, as you guessed, this is dispiriting. For one thing, it bores me to see my supposed "profession" reduced to recycling. Nobody ever even has the originality to say "Hitchens, who criticised Mother Teresa for her warm endorsement of the Duvalier regime in Haiti." This is the surreptitious way in which dissenting views are marginalised, or patronised to death. However, it wasn't self-pity that prompted me to write. Let me tell you what happened to me in the course of a single month, between May and June of 2001.

At the direct request of the Vatican, I was invited to give evidence for the opposing side in the hearings on Mother Teresa's impending canonisation. It was an astonishing opportunity to play Devil's Advocate in the literal sense, and I must say that the Church behaved with infinitely more care and scruple than my liberal critics. A closed room, a Bible, a tape-recorder, a Monsignor, a Deacon and a Father—a solemn exercise in deposition, where I was encouraged to produce all my findings and opinions. I'll tell you all about it at another time; the point is that the record is not now the monopoly of the fundamentalists.

British television broadcast an exhaustive documentary on Princess Diana, giving (at last) proper space and time to those of us who did not subscribe to her cult. I was interviewed at some length, and didn't receive a fraction of the hysterical mailbag that was, not long ago, an occupational hazard. Who could make that soufflé rise twice?

Slobodan Milosevic was taken to the Hague to face a tribunal. I didn't exactly rejoice at the way he was effectively "bought" from Serbia in exchange for promises of financial aid, but it is some years now since he undertook at Dayton to cooperate with the tribunal, and enough was enough. I thought of all the arguments I'd had about Srebrenica and Sarajevo and Kosovo, and all the half-baked excuses that had been offered for doing nothing to stop Serbo-fascism, and all the times in Bosnia when the situation had seemed hopeless, and allowed myself to be quietly proud of what little I'd done, as well as ashamed by how little that was.

Bill Clinton's approving Presidential initials were found on a note written by his half-brother Roger, who had been engaged in trying to obtain a pardon for a drug-dealer and also engaged in explaining how he'd come by a brick-thick block of traveler's checks. There was the usual obfuscation about "no proven quid pro quo" but I noticed, in the aftermath of the Rich pardon, that it had been several months since I'd been able to get into a fight over whether Clinton was a cheap crook or not. Believe me, I remember when this was otherwise....

Henry Kissinger, challenged on television to meet my accusation that he was responsible for war crimes and crimes against humanity, responded with a maniacal and desperate attempt to change the subject, and denounced me as a denier of the Nazi Holocaust. (He also followed custom in mentioning Mother Teresa and, for some reason, Jackie Kennedy.) This enabled me to bring legal proceedings against him, both for defamation in my own case and – via the discovery process – to demonstrate that he was a practised and habitual liar. Considering what I had said about him in print, the disproportion between my suing him and him suing me was evident to all. But I could prove that what I said was true, whereas he could not, and that is still a difference. (Adlai Stevenson once said to Richard Nixon: "If you stop telling lies about me I'll stop telling the truth about you." I like the euphony, but I'd have no right to make such a bargain with the man who devastated Cambodia and Cyprus and Chile and East Timor.)

So this was an amazing and wondrous month; perhaps the best of my life. (I finished my centennial study of George Orwell in the same period. Much more civilised to be writing about him than any of the above.) I tell you about it not just in order to boast, though there is that. It went to make up for many, many other months, when the celebrity culture and the spin-scum and the crooked lawyers and pseudo-statesmen and clerics seemed to have everything their own way. They will be back, of course. They are always "back". They never leave. But their victory is not pre-determined. And there are vindications to be had as well, far sweeter than anything contained in the meretricious illusion of good notices or "a good press".

I hope I shall be able to reinforce some of this in the following pages, which I once again thank you for provoking me to write.

— Christopher Hitchens
Stanford, California
Independence Day 2001

▨ Introduction

The ensuing pages represent my tentative acceptance of
a challenge that was made to me in the early months of
the year 2000. Could I offer any advice to the young and
the restless; any counsel that would help them avoid dis-
illusionment? Among my students at the New School in
New York, and in the bars and cafes of the other cam-
puses where I spoke, there were many who retained the
unfashionable hope of changing the world for the better
and (which is not quite the same thing) of living a life
that would be, as far as possible, self-determined. This
conversation had taken many forms over the years, until
I began to feel the weight of every millisecond that
marked me as a grizzled soixante-huitard, or survivor of
the last intelligible era of revolutionary upheaval, the
one that partly ended and partly culminated in les evene-
ments de quatre-vingt neuf. Then came the proposal to
state and discuss the matter in epistolary form; to be spe-
cific, the form suggested by Rainer Maria Rilke in his
Letters to a Young Poet. My immediate reaction was to
recall what Byron said in his poem of reproach to the
servile Greeks:

And shall thy lyre, so long divine,
Degenerate into hands like mine?

However, various of my students thought it might be worthwhile, or at least potentially amusing, and the following letters are written to one of them in distilled form, as if he/she represented them all.

letters to a
young contrarian

I

My dear X,

So then—you rather tend to flatter and embarrass me, when you inquire my advice as to how a radical or "contrarian" life may be lived. The flattery is in your suggestion that I might be anybody's "model," when almost by definition a single existence cannot furnish any pattern (and, if it is lived in dissent, should not anyway be supposed to be emulated). The embarrassment lies in the very title that you propose. It is a strange thing, but it remains true that our language and culture contain no proper word for your aspiration. The noble title of "dissident" must be earned rather than claimed; it connotes sacrifice and risk rather than mere disagreement, and it has been consecrated by many exemplary and courageous men and women. "Radical" is a useful and honorable term—in many ways it's my preferred one—but it comes with various health warnings that I'll discuss with you in a later missive. Our remaining expressions— "maverick," "loose cannon," "rebel," "angry young man," "gadfly"—are all slightly affectionate and diminutive and are, perhaps for that reason, somewhat condescending. It can be understood from them that society, like a benign family, tolerates and even admires eccentricity. Even the term "Iconoclast" is seldom used negatively, but rather to suggest that the breaking of images is a harmless discharge of energy. There even exist official phrases of approbation for this tendency, of which the latest is the supposedly praiseworthy ability to "think outside the box." I myself hope to live long enough to graduate, from being a "bad boy"—which I once was—to becoming "a curmudgeon." And then "the enormous condescension of posterity"—a rather suggestive phrase minted by E.P. Thompson, a heretic who was a veteran when I was but a lad—may cover my bones.

Go too far outside "the box," of course, and you will encounter a vernacular that is much less "tolerant." Here, the key words are "fanatic," "troublemaker," "misfit" or "malcontent." In between we can find numberless self-congratulatory memoirs, with generic titles such as *Against the Stream*, or *Against the Current*. (Harold Rosenberg, writing about his fellow "New York intellectuals," once gave this school the collective name of "the herd of independent minds.")

Meanwhile, the ceaseless requirements of the entertainment industry also threaten to deprive us of other forms of critical style, and of the means of appreciating them. To be called "satirical" or "ironic" is now to be patronised in a different way; the satirist is the fast-talking cynic and the ironist merely sarcastic or self-conscious and wised-up. When a precious and irreplaceable word like "irony" has become a lazy synonym for "anomie," there is scant room for originality.

However, let us not repine. It's too much to expect to live in an age that is actually *propitious* for dissent. And most people, most of the time, prefer to seek approval or security. Nor should this surprise us (and nor, incidentally, are those desires contemptible in themselves). Nonetheless, there are in all periods people who feel themselves in some fashion to be *apart*. And it is not too much to say that humanity is very much in debt to such people, whether it chooses to acknowledge the debt or not. (Don't expect to be thanked, by the way. The life of an oppositionist is supposed to be difficult.)

I nearly hit upon the word "dissenter" just now, which might do as a definition if it were not for certain religious and sectarian connotations. The same problem arises with "freethinker." But the latter term is probably the superior one, since it makes an essential point about thinking for oneself. The essence of the independent mind lies not in *what* it thinks, but in *how* it thinks. The term "intellectual" was originally coined by those in France who believed in the guilt of Captain Alfred Dreyfus. They thought that they were defending an organic, harmonious and ordered society against nihilism, and they deployed this contemptuous word against those they regarded as the diseased, the introspective, the disloyal and the unsound. The word hasn't completely lost this association even now, though it is less frequently used as an insult. (And, like "Tory," "impressionist" and "suffragette," all of them originated as terms of abuse or scorn, it has been annexed by some of its targets and worn with pride.) One feels something of the same sense of embarrassment in claiming to be an "intellectual" as one does in purporting to be a dissident, but the figure of Emile Zola offers encouragement, and his singular campaign for justice is one of the imperishable examples of what may be accomplished by an individual.

Zola did not in fact require much intellectual capacity to mount his defense of one wronged man. He applied, first, the forensic and journalistic skills that he was used to employing for the social background of his novels. These put him in the possession of the unarguable facts. But the mere facts were not sufficient, because the anti-Dreyfusards did not base their real case on the actual guilt or innocence of the defendant. They openly maintained that, for reasons of state, it was better not to reopen the case. Such a reopening would only serve to dissipate public confidence in order and in institutions. Why take this risk at all? And why on earth take it on behalf of a Jew? The partisans of Dreyfus therefore had to face the accusation not that they were mistaken as to the facts, but that they were treacherous, unpatriotic and irreligious; accusations which tended to keep some prudent people out of the fray.

There is a saying from Roman antiquity: *Fiat justitia—ruat caelum*. "Do justice, and let the skies fall." In every epoch, there have been those to argue that "greater" goods, such as tribal solidarity or social cohesion, take precedence over the demands of justice. It is supposed to be an axiom of "Western" civilisation that the individual, or the truth, may not be sacrificed to hypothetical benefits such as "order." But in point of fact, such immolations have been very common. To the extent that the ideal is at least paid lip service, this result is the outcome of individual struggles against the collective instinct for a quiet life. Emile Zola could be the pattern for any serious and humanistic radical, because he not only asserted the inalienable rights of the individual, but generalised his assault to encompass the vile role played by clericalism, by racial hatred, by militarism and by the fetishisation of "the nation" and the state. His caustic and brilliant epistolary campaign of 1897 and 1898 may be read as a curtain-raiser for most of the great contests that roiled the coming twentieth century.

People forget that, before he addressed his most celebrated letter, *J'Accuse*, to the president of the Republic, Zola had also issued open letters to the youth of France, and to France itself. He did not confine himself to excoriating the corrupted elite, but held up a mirror in which public opinion could see its own ugliness reflected. To the young people he wrote, after recalling the braver days when the Latin Quarter had been ablaze with sympathy for Poland and Greece, of his disgust with the students who had demonstrated against the Dreyfusards:

> *Anti-Semites among our young men? They do exist then, do they? This idiotic poison has really already overthrown their intellects and corrupted their souls?*

What a saddening, what a disquieting element for the twentieth century which is about to dawn. A hundred years after the Declaration of the Rights of Man, a hundred years after the supreme act of tolerance and emancipation, we go back to religious warfare, to the most odious and the most stupid of fanaticisms!

Describing the sick moral atmosphere, Zola used a striking image:

A shameful terror reigns, the bravest turn cowards, and no one dares say what he thinks for fear of being denounced as a traitor and a bribe-taker. The few newspapers which at first stood out for justice are now crawling in the dust before their readers . . .

He returned to this theme in his letter to the French nation, asking his fellow citizens to consider:

Are you aware that the danger lies precisely in this somber obstinacy of public opinion? A hundred newspapers repeat daily that public opinion does not wish the innocence of Dreyfus, that his guilt is necessary to the safety of the country. And do you know to what point you yourself will be guilty, should those in authority take advantage of such a sophism to stifle the truth?

Never one to be abstract in his analysis of society, Zola exposed the almost sadomasochistic relationship that existed between insecure mobs and their adulation of "strong men" and the military:

> *Examine your conscience. Was it in truth your Army which you wished to defend when none were attacking it? Was it not rather the sword that you felt the sudden need of extolling?*
>
> *At bottom, yours is not yet the real republican blood; the sight of a plumed helmet still makes your heart beat quicker, no king can come amongst us but you fall in love with him. . . . It is not of your Army that you are thinking, but of the General who happens to have caught your fancy.*

Finest of all in my opinion was Zola's direct and measured indictment of the complicity of the Church:

> *And do you know where else you walk, France? You go to the Church of Rome, you return to that past of intolerance and theocracy against which the greatest of your children fought. . . . Today, the tactics of the anti-Semites are very simple. Catholicism, seeking in vain to influence the people, founded workmen's clubs and multiplied pilgrimages; it failed to win them back or lead them again to the foot of the altar. The question seemed definitely settled, the churches remained empty, the people had lost their faith. And behold, circumstances have occurred which make it possible to infect them with an anti-Semitic fury, and having*

7

> *been poisoned with this virus of fanaticism, they are*
> *launched upon the streets to shout "Down with the*
> *Jews! Death to the Jews!". . . When the people of*
> *France have been changed into fanatics and torturers,*
> *when their generosity and love of the rights of man,*
> *conquered with so much difficulty, have been rooted up*
> *out of their hearts, then no doubt God will do the rest.*

This was *saeva indignatio* of a quality not seen since Swift himself. So that by the time Zola addressed himself, on the front page of *L'Aurore*, to President Felix Faure he was only completing the details of his bill of indictment, and accusing a syndicate of reactionaries of committing a double crime—that of framing an innocent man and acquitting a guilty one. (It's always as well to remember, when considering "miscarriages" of justice, as the authorities so neutrally and quaintly like to call them, that the framing of the innocent axiomatically involves the exculpation of the guilty. This is abortion, not miscarriage.)

Read Zola with care and you will be less astonished by the follies and crimes—from Verdun to Vichy—that later overtook France, and indeed overtook an entire Europe of show trials and camps and martial parades and infallible leaders. You will also understand better why it is that the papacy, which now seems to try again almost every day, can never manage an honest or clear statement on its history with Jews, Protestants and unbelievers. And all of this can be derived from one determined and principled individual exercising his right to say no, and insisting (as Zola successfully did) on his day, not "in court" as we again too neutrally say, but in the dock.

Another observation from antiquity has it that, while courage is not in itself one of the primary virtues, it is the quality that makes the exercise of the virtues possible. Again, this removes it from the strict province of the "intellectual." Galileo may have made a discovery that overthrew the complacent cosmology of the Church fathers, but when threatened with the instruments of torture he also made a swift recantation. The sun and the planets were, of course, unaffected by this disavowal, and the latter continued to revolve around the former whatever the Vatican said. (Galileo himself, as he finished his recantation, may or may not have murmured, *"epur si muove"*—"It still does move.")

But he furnishes us with an example of objective-free inquiry, rather than of heretical courage. Others had to be courageous on his behalf, as Zola had to be brave on behalf of Dreyfus. (Incidentally, it now seems more and more certain that Zola was murdered in his bed, rather than accidentally stifled by a faulty fire and a blocked chimney; further proof that great men are most frequently not honored in their own time or country.)

I think often of my late friend Ron Ridenhour, who became briefly famous when, as an American serviceman in Vietnam, he collected and exposed the evidence of the hideous massacre of the villagers at My Lai in

March 1968. One of the hardest things for anyone to face is the conclusion that his or her "own" side is in the wrong when engaged in a war. The pressure to keep silent and be a "team player" is reinforceable by the accusations of cowardice or treachery that will swiftly be made against dissenters. Sinister phrases of coercion, such as "stabbing in the back" or "giving ammunition to the enemy," have their origin in this dilemma and are always available to help compel unanimity. For resisting this, and for insisting that American officers and men be bound by the customary laws of war, Ron Ridenhour put many people in safer positions to shame. It probably helped, as he once told me, that he himself was the son of a poor white Arizona good ol' boy family, rather than a bookish or pointy-headed bleeding heart. It all began, in his recollection, when as an uneducated draftee he was lying in his bunk and overheard a group of fellow enlisted men planning a nighttime assault on the only black soldier in the hut. Ron said that he sat up in his own bunk, and heard himself saying, "If you want to do that, you have to come through me." As so often, the determination of one individual was enough to dishearten those whose courage was mob-derived. But remember, until the crucial moment arrived he had no idea that he was going to behave in this way.

In my life I have had the privilege and luck of meeting and interviewing a number of brave dissidents in many and various countries and societies. Very frequently, they can trace their careers (which partly "chose" them rather than being chosen by them) to an incident in early life where they felt obliged to make or take a stand. Sometimes, too, a precept is offered and takes root. Bertrand Russell in his *Autobiography* records that his rather fearsome Puritan grandmother "gave me a Bible with her favourite texts written on the fly-leaf. Among these was 'Thou shalt not follow a multitude to do evil.' Her emphasis upon this text led me in later life to be not afraid of belonging to small minorities." It's rather affecting to find the future hammer of the Christians being "confirmed" in this way. It also proves that sound maxims can appear in the least probable places.

Quite often, the "baptism" of a future dissenter occurs in something unplanned, such as a spontaneous resistance to an episode of bullying or bigotry, or a challenge to some piece of pedagogical stupidity. There is good reason to think that such reactions arise from something innate rather than something inculcated: Nickleby doesn't know until the moment of the crisis that he is going to stick up for poor Smike. Noam Chomsky recalls hearing the news of the obliteration of Hiroshima as a young man, and experiencing the need to go off and find solitude because there was nobody he felt he could talk to. It would be encouraging to believe that such reactions *are* innate, because then we can be certain that they will continue to occur, and will not depend for their occurrence upon the transmission of good examples or morality tales.

It may be that you, my dear X, recognise something of yourself in these instances; a disposition to resistance, however slight, against arbitrary authority or witless mass opinion, or a thrill of recognition when you encounter some well-wrought phrase from a free intelligence. If so, let us continue to correspond so that I may draw from your experience even as you flatter me by asking to draw upon mine. For the moment, do bear in mind that the cynics have a point, of a sort, when they speak of the "professional nay-sayer." To be in opposition is not to be a nihilist. And there is no decent or charted way of making a living at it. It is something you are, and not something you do.

II

I think the proposal to be guided by Rilke is a delightful one, because it starts me off in company I have no right to claim, and in the sort of company that I do not ordinarily keep. It also gives me something to react against. Of course I admire the exquisite delicacy of Rilke's letters, even though their polished manners and considerate, courteous tone strike me as too lenient. (It's fairly clear that the verses he was being shown were not much good, and he could have been more emphatic in saying so.) Moreover, the letters breathe with that atmosphere of slightly sickly innocence that wafts toward us from the days immediately before 1914. (George Dangerfield deals with it trenchantly, especially in its epicene Rupert Brooke–ish mode, in his magnificent book *The Strange Death of Liberal England*, which I commend highly to you.)

A similar objection can be registered to some of Rilke's poetry and prose, which exhibits that species of German romanticism and idealism that I find suspect even in the most scrupulous hands. I am always and at once on the defensive, for example, when people speak of races and nations as if they were personalities and had souls and destinies and suchlike. Furthermore, Rilke's attitude to the religio-spiritual life seems sentimental to me. It is true that he learned, from his master Auguste Rodin, the idea that art can be a religious activity and that poetry can aim to be as exact as sculpture. But it would be better to go back and read Spinoza in the original than to be satisfied with this slightly precious secondhand version of it.

In his own life, Rilke illustrated some of the sinister side of romantic idealism. He fell for the allure of Mussolini, for example, as did D'Annunzio and Marinetti and other quasi-aesthetes. He detested psychoanalysis and hated Freud in particular (his private letters showing him as something less than a philo-Semite). Above all—and this is an acid test for me—he was suspicious of irony. As he wrote to his young correspondent:

> *Don't let yourself be controlled by it, especially during uncreative moments. When you are fully creative, try to use it, as one more way to take hold of life. Used purely, it too is pure, and one needn't be ashamed of it; but if you feel yourself becoming too familiar with it, if you are afraid of this growing familiarity, then turn to great and serious objects, in front of which it becomes small and helpless. Search into the depth of Things: there, irony never descends—and when you arrive at the edge of greatness, find out whether this way of perceiving the world arises from a necessity of your being. For*

under the influence of serious Things it will either
fall away from you (if it is something accidental), or
else, (if it is really innate and belongs to you) it will
grow strong, and become a serious tool and take its
place among the instruments which you can form
your art with.

It may be my Englishness, but this strenuous Capital-
isation of the Abstract, and this allied tendency to tautology, remind me instantly of the moment in Evelyn
Waugh's novella *The Loved One* where an advice colum-
nist is asked for help in combatting nail biting and asks
his assistant: "What did we tell her last time?" "Medita-
tion on the Beautiful." "Tell her to go on meditating."
Irony is not as easily relegated as that. (Rilke then goes
on to confide in us rather archly about the only two
works from which he is never parted: "the Bible and the
books of the great Danish poet Jens Peter Jacobsen."
This piety somewhat spoils the recommendation of *Niels
Lyhne*, Jacobsen's excellent novel, which was rightly ad-
mired by Freud and by Thomas Mann and which is a sort
of Danish *Young Werther*.)

As against this, we have Rilke's astonishingly percep-
tive if slightly overwrought advice to the aspiring writer:

There is only one thing you should do. Go into yourself.
Find out the reason that commands you to write; see
whether it has spread its roots into the very depths of
your heart; confess to yourself whether you would have

> *to die if you were forbidden to write. This most of all;*
> *ask yourself in the most silent hour of your night: must*
> *I write? Dig into yourself for a deep answer. And if*
> *this answer rings out in assent, if you meet this*
> *question with a strong, simple "I must," then build*
> *your life in accordance with this necessity . . .*

With much less eloquence, this is what I have been telling writing classes for years. You must feel not that you *want* to but that you *have* to. It's worth emphasising, too, because there is a relationship, inexact to be sure but a relationship, between this desire or need and the ambition to rely upon internal exile, or dissent; the decision to live at a slight acute angle to society.

The other positive and affirmative element in Rilke is his approach to Eros. He had a high intuition about sex, both as a liberating force and also as the best riposte to the foul suggestions of death. His seven so-called Phallic Poems are among the best non–love verses since the brave days of Marvell and the Metaphysicals; they openly announce that fucking is its own justification. He's more guarded about this in the *Letters* but Rodin would have been proud; there is sculpting going on in those poems. The fact that they were written during the second winter of the First World War is not coincidental; Thanatos was rampant in those days (as Rilke understood, seeing the advent of the war as a calamity for civilisation) and something had to be said and done about it. His solutions were to propose sexual passion in private and, in public, to affirm both his Slavic identity as a German born in Prague and his cosmopolitan identity as a German who could enrage the Uhland types by writing in the decadent tongue of France. This makes his later fatuities about fascism even harder to bear.

But contradiction is of the essence: many of my own favorite poets in English, from Kipling to Larkin, have achieved great and splendid effects in spite of, as well as because of, their affinity with ethical conservatism, sometimes in its radical forms. I accept all of Rilke's implied challenges because of what he wrote about *solitude*, and the ways in which it must be welcomed rather than feared. In the mental and moral equipment of a radical or critical personality, this realisation is of the essence. Rilke also allows me to touch on matters such as the inevitable disappointment of religion and worship, the defining importance of language, the combat between the tribal and the cosmopolitan, the fate of *MittelEuropa*, the still-poisonous influence of the First World War, the effect of Freud, and the recurring importance of the ironic. This is enough to be going on with.

III

Your last letter reached me just as I was reading the essays of Aldous Huxley, creator of our notion of a "Brave New World." Allow me to give you a paragraph that I marked as I went along:

"Homer was wrong," wrote Heracleitus of Ephesus. "Homer was wrong in saying: 'Would that strife might perish from among gods and men!' He did not see that he was praying for the destruction of the universe; for if his prayer were heard, all things would pass away." These are words on which the superhumanists should meditate. Aspiring toward a consistent perfection, they are aspiring toward annihilation. The Hindus had the wit to see and the courage to proclaim the fact; Nirvana, the goal of their striving, is nothingness. Wherever life exists, there also is inconsistency, division, strife.

You seem to have grasped the point that there is something idiotic about those who believe that consensus (to give the hydra-headed beast just one of its names) is the highest good. Why do I use the offensive word "idiotic"? For two reasons that seem good to me; the first being my conviction that human beings do not, in fact, desire to live in some Disneyland of the mind, where there is an end to striving and a general feeling of contentment and bliss. This would be idiocy in its pejorative sense; the Athenians originally employed the term more lightly, defining as *idiotis* any man who was blandly indifferent to public affairs.

My second reason is less intuitive. Even if we did really harbor this desire, it would fortunately be unattainable. As a species, we may by all means think ruefully about the waste and horror produced by war and other forms of rivalry and jealousy. However, this can't alter the fact that in life we make progress by conflict and in mental life by argument and disputation. The concept of the dialectic may well have been partly discredited by its advocates, but that does not permit us to disown it. There must be confrontation and opposition, in order that sparks may be kindled. You have probably heard, from one complacent pundit or another, the view that argument produces "more heat than light." You have certainly been instructed that truth lies not at one pole or another but "somewhere in between." And I think I can be sure that you have heard the good old standby, to the effect that matters are not black or white, but differing shades of gray.

May I offer you some observations of my own in response? We know as a law of physics that heat is the chief, if not the only, source of light. Reducing the sun to room temperature would decrease light to nothing at all, as well as generating a definite chill. The truth cannot lie, but if it could, it would lie somewhere in between. On some grave questions, there is no difference to be split; one does not look for a synthesis between verity and falsehood; the sun does not rise in the east one day and in the west the next. As for the *chiaroscuro*, or the light and shade, the platitude is at least a little more artistic. (Watching a Civil War reenactment at Gettysburg a few years ago, I wrote in my notebook that those who wore the Gray had been conditioned to think in terms of black and white.) Neither black nor white are true colors, but then neither is gray.

Tautology lurks, and waits to enclose you. The Greek oracle proclaimed "Nothing Too Much" as the supreme wisdom; the lazy modern translation is "Moderation in All Things," which is not quite the same. One admires the Greek style for its quiet emphasis on symmetry and balance, but then what if the balance is tipped and the time disjointed? Of what use is the "moderate" then? The Gray uniforms at Gettysburg might not have been deployed, or not have been defeated, if it were not for fanatics and absolutists like John Brown, who regarded compromise as disgrace. No doubt you can think of your own examples.

If you care about the points of agreement and civility, then, you had better be well-equipped with points of argument and combativity, because if you are not then the "center" will be occupied and defined without your having helped to decide it, or determine what and where it is. That is, unless you trust the transcendent sapience of the Dalai Lama, whose work I was reading in parallel to

Huxley's. Here is what the enlightened one told his interlocutor, at the opening of *The Art of Happiness: A Handbook for Living*, an extensive and best-selling transcription of his own words:

> *I believe that the very purpose of our life is to seek happiness. That is clear. Whether one believes in religion or not, whether one believes in this religion or that religion, we all are seeking something better in life. So, I think, the very motion of our life is towards happiness.*

This is how the Dalai Lama began his address "to a large audience in Arizona." The very best that can be said is that he uttered a string of fatuous non sequiturs. There is not even a strand of chewing gum to connect the premise to the conclusion; the speaker simply assumes what he has to prove. The odd thing is that in the last sentence the words "I think" are inserted, as if in compliment to the old-fashioned and materialist notion that the human brain might have a say. I once spent some time in an ashram in Poona, outside Bombay. I was posing as an acolyte in order to make a BBC documentary about the then-guru Bhagwan Shree Rajneesh, who had built himself a large and lucrative practise among well-off Westerners and minor European royalty. The whole thing was a racket of course—the divine purveyor of disco philosophy had the world's largest private collection of Rolls-Royces—but what I remember best was the morning *darshan* with the all-wise. On the way into the assembly one had to be sniffed from head to toe by two agonisingly beautiful California girls dressed in flame-ochre kimonos. This was to protect the Bhagwan from the material fact that, as his disciples put it, "his body has a few allergies." The lovely sniffers were supposed to detect any traces of alcohol or tobacco. And every morning, redolent as I must have been, I passed their exacting test. But what made me personally allergic, each roseate dawn, was the large sign posted at the point where footwear had to be discarded. "Shoes and minds," said this sign, "must be left at the gate." Laughable of course, but evil if it could be enforced, as it often was under Loyola's Jesuitical injunction *Dei sacrificium intellectus*; an immodest and hysterical desire to annihilate the intellect at the feet of an idol.

It's often been observed that the major religions can give no convincing account of Paradise. They do much better in representing Hell; indeed one of the early Christian dogmatists, Tertullian, borrowed the vividness of the latter to lend point to the former. Among the delights of Heaven, he decided, would be the contemplation of the tortures of the damned. This anthropomorphism at least had a bit of bite to it; the problem in all the other cases is that nobody can seriously desire the dissolution of the intellect. And the pleasures and rewards of the intellect are inseparable from *angst*, uncertainty, conflict and even despair.

I am sure that you can see where I am hoping to take you. I want to reserve the question of religion and faith for a later exchange between us, but you did ask me, after my last letter, to say whether I had undergone any early formative experience of my own. Well, the answer is yes, even though the episode is trivial. I was sitting in a bible-study class at the age of about ten ("divinity," as we called it, being as mandatory as daily church attendance, and one of my favorite subjects then as now) when the teacher began to hymn the work of god in Nature. How wonderful it was, she said, that trees and vegetation were green; the most restful color to our eyes. Imagine if instead the woods and grasses were purple, or orange. I knew nothing about chlorophyll and phototropism at that age, still less about the Argument from Design or the debate on Creationism versus Evolution. I merely remember thinking, with my childish and unformed cortex: Oh, don't be silly.

It's for this reason that I am quite sure of two things. The first is that even uneducated people, whether sunk in the theocratic despotisms of yore, or the more modernised totalitarianisms of today (or the other way about, if you prefer) have an innate capacity to resist and, if not even to think for themselves, to have thoughts occur to them. We know this empirically, because such people always appear as if from nowhere when despotisms fall. But I also believe that we can know it by induction.

The second, which is only a corollary of the first, is that we do not naturally aspire to any hazy, narcotic Nirvana, where our critical and ironic faculties would be of no use to us. Imagine a state of endless praise and gratitude and adoration, as the Testaments ceaselessly enjoin us to do, and you have conjured a world of hellish nullity and conformism. Imagine a state of bliss and perpetual happiness and harmony, and you have summoned a vision of tedium and pointlessness and predictability, such as Huxley with all his gifts was only able to sketch. Only one other sacred text mentions "happiness" without embarrassment. But even in 1776, this concept was thought to be mentionable only as the consequence of a bitter struggle, just then being embarked upon. The beautiful word "pursuit," however we construe it, would be vacuous in any other context.

I close by saying, as I may well have occasion to say again: Always look to the language.

IV

I was most heartened to have your reply. It is true that the odds in favor of stupidity or superstition or unchecked authority seem intimidating and that vast stretches of human time have seemingly elapsed with no successful challenge to these things. But it is no less true that there is an ineradicable instinct to see beyond, or through, these tyrannical conditions. One way of phrasing it might be to say that injustice and irrationality are inevitable parts of the human condition, but that challenges to them are inevitable also. On Sigmund Freud's memorial in Vienna appear the words: "The voice of reason is small, but very persistent." Philosophers and theologians have cogitated or defined this in differing ways, postulating that we respond to a divinely implanted "conscience" or that—as Adam Smith had it—we carry around an unseen witness to our thoughts and doings, and seek to make a good impression on this worthy bystander. Neither assumption need be valid; it's enough that we know that this innate spirit exists. We have to add the qualification, however, that even if it is presumptively latent in all of us it very often remains just that—latent. Its existence guarantees nothing in itself, and the catalytic or Promethean moment only occurs when one individual is prepared to cease being the passive listener to such a voice, and to become instead its spokesman, or representative.

You ask me for some encouraging examples. I don't wish to furnish the sort of slogan that might appear on some cheery poster or be used as some uplifting motto. Again, it is a matter of how one thinks and not of what one thinks. However, there are some flashes of human intelligence that rise above the merely contrary, and that can show us how some of our predecessors dealt with fiercer opposition than we face at present.

Alain, in Martin du Gard's *Lieutenant Colonel Maumort* says that the first rule—he calls it the rule of rules—is the art of challenging what is appealing. You will notice that he describes this as an "art": it is not enough simply to set oneself up as a person who distrusts majority taste as a matter of principle or perhaps conceit; that way lies snobbery and frigidity. However, it will very often be found that people are highly attached to illusions or prejudices, and are not just the sullen victims of dogma or orthodoxy. If you have ever argued with a religious devotee, for example, you will have noticed that his self-esteem and pride are involved in the dispute, and that you are asking him to give up something more than a point in argument. The same is true of visceral patriots, and admirers of monarchy and aristocracy. Allegiance is a powerful force in human affairs; it will not do to treat someone as a mental serf if he is convinced that his thralldom is honorable and voluntary.

From this caution I pass to an observation of the late Sir Karl Popper, who could himself be a tyrant in argument but who nonetheless recognised that argument was valuable, indeed essential, *for its own sake.* It is very seldom, as he noticed, that in debate any one of two evenly matched antagonists will succeed in actually convincing or "converting" the other. But it is equally seldom that in a properly conducted argument either antagonist will end up holding exactly the same position as that with which he began. Concessions, refinements and adjustments will occur, and each initial position will have undergone modification even if it remains ostensibly the "same." Not even the most apparently glacial "system" is immune to this rule. ("*Plus c'est la meme chose,*" as Isaac Deutscher presciently said of the old and calcified Soviet Union, *"plus ca change."*)

It is striking how often the masters in this art have repeated each other's discoveries. George Orwell said that the prime responsibility lay in being able to tell people what they did not wish to hear. John Stuart Mill (who by a nice chance was Bertrand Russell's godfather) said that even if all were agreed on an essential proposition it would be essential to give an ear to the one person who did not, lest people forget how to justify their original agreement. Karl Marx, asked to give his favorite epigram, offered *de omnibus disputandum* ("everything must be doubted"). A pity that so many of his followers forgot the pith of this saying. Rosa Luxemburg roundly declared that freedom was first and last the freedom for those who thought differently. John Milton in his *Areopagitica* proclaimed that, whatever one believed to be the right, it should be exposed to the claims of the wrong, because only in a fair and open fight could the right claim or expect vindication. Frederick Douglass announced that those who expected truth or justice without a struggle were like those who could imagine the sea without an image of the tempest.

These perceptions are not being offered by me to you for the benefit of those who have not yet appreciated them. *De te fabula narratur*. This story is about you: at your own peril you forget how much you have to learn rather than teach by taking such a stand. The presumed educator must be educated. I have a dear friend in Jerusalem, that home of rectitude and certainty that is so often presented to us as "holy" for no better reason than its unenviable position as "home" to three (highly schismatic but self-described) "mono"theisms. His name is Dr. Israel Shahak; for many years he did exemplary service as chairman of the Israeli League for Human and Civil Rights. Nothing in his life, as a Jewish youth in pre–1940 Poland and subsequent survivor of indescribable privations and losses, might be expected to have conditioned him to welcome the disruptive. Yet on some occasions when I have asked him for his impression of events, he has calmly and deliberately replied: "There are some encouraging signs of polarisation." Nothing flippant inheres in this remark; a long and risky life has persuaded him that only an open conflict of ideas and principles can produce any clarity. Conflict may be painful, but the painless solution does not exist in any case and the pursuit of it leads to the painful outcome of mindlessness and pointlessness; the apotheosis of the ostrich.

Contrast this to the unashamed recommendations of the mindless that are offered to us every day. In place of honest disputation we are offered platitudes about "healing." The idea of "unity" is granted huge privileges over any notion of "division" or, worse, "divisiveness." I cringe every time I hear denunciations of "the politics of division"—as if politics was not division by definition. Semi-educated people join cults whose whole purpose is to dull the pain of thought, or take medications that claim to abolish anxiety. Oriental religions, with their emphasis on Nirvana and fatalism, are repackaged for Westerners as therapy, and platitudes or tautologies masquerade as wisdom. (Anthony Powell, in his marvellous novel sequence *A Dance to the Music of Time*, captures the foolishness of such mantras very well in his depiction of the followers of the sinister Dr. Trelawney. Adepts of his cult recognise each other by the greeting: "The essence of the all is the godhead of the true" and by the response: "The vision of visions heals the blindness of sight." I think of this whenever I hear babble about the Ultimate, the Absolute, the Beyond and other regions where the cerebral cortex has surrendered itself to dissipation.)

A map of the world that does not include Utopia, said Oscar Wilde, is not worth glancing at. A noble sentiment, and a good thrust at the Gradgrinds and utilitarians. Bear in mind, however, that Utopia itself was a tyranny and that much of the talk about the analgesic and conflict-free ideal is likewise more menacing than it may appear. These Ultimates and Absolutes are attempts at Perfection, which is—so to speak—a latently Absolutist idea. (You should scan Brian Victoria's excellent book *Zen at War*, which, written as it is by a Buddhist priest, exposes the dire role played by Zen obedience and discipline in the formation of pre-war Japanese imperialism.)

In rejecting Perfectionism, I don't want you to fall into the opposite error, which is that of taking human nature just as you find it. My friend Basil Davidson, who wrote a splendid memoir of his years with the anti-Nazi partisan fighters in the Balkans, concluded from his experience that it was wrong to endorse the lazy proposition that "You can't change human nature." At first hand, he said, he had seen it become changed—for the worse. Ought not the corollary to hold—that if it can be altered one way it can surely be altered the other? Not necessarily: we are mammals, and the prefrontal lobe (at least while we wait for genetic engineering) is too small while the adrenaline gland is too big. Nonetheless, civilisation can increase, and at times actually has increased, the temptation to behave in a civilised way. It is only those who hope to *transform* humans who end up by burning them, like the waste product of a failed experiment.

Perfectionists and zealots can break but not bend; in my experience they are subject to burnout from diminishing returns or else, to borrow Santayana's definition of the fanatic, they redouble their efforts just when they have lost sight of their ends. If you find yourself, as Basil Davidson did, in mortal conflict with a hateful foreign occupation, then you can be forgiven for being a zealot and even criticised for not being one. Such cruel tests are rare, however, and they can produce horrors in their turn. If you want to stay in for the long haul, and lead a life that is free from illusions either propagated by you or embraced by you, then I suggest you learn to recognise and avoid the symptoms of the zealot and the person who *knows* that he is right. For the dissenter, the skeptical mentality is at least as important as any armor of principle.

V

Now you ask me, to what purpose is such a life to be devoted? In a way, you miss my point, since I believe (and I hope I argued) that such a life is worth living on its own account. But perhaps this merely betrays the ageing process at work upon me. I mentioned earlier the irritating term or tag "Angry Young Man," with which awkward types are put in their place as callow young rebels going through a "phase." In *Look Back in Anger*, the mediocre play by John Osborne that gave currency to the usage, the protagonist Jimmy Porter is going through one of his self-regarding soliloquies when he exclaims, rather tellingly for once, that there are "no more good, brave causes left." This utterance struck home in the consciousness of the mid-1950s, at a time when existential anomie was trading at an inflated price.

Within a few years, I need not add, millions of young people had forsaken the Absurd in order to engage with such good, if not invariably brave, causes as the Civil Rights movement, the struggle against thermonuclear statism, and the ending of an unjust war in Indochina. I was myself "of" this period, and have witnessed some truly marvellous moments at firsthand. (I shan't tell you

my stories unless you specifically request them; I know
that nothing is more tedious than the front-line recollec-
tions of a Sixties radical.)

Nobody in the supposedly affluent and disillusioned
fifties had seen any of this coming; I am quite certain
that there will be future opportunities for people of
high ideals, or of any ideals at all. However, in the fairly
long interval between 1968 and 1989—in other words
in that period where many of the revolutionaries against
consumer capitalism metamorphosed into "civil society" human-rights activists—there were considerable
interludes of quietism and stasis. And it was in order to
survive those years of stalemate and *realpolitik* that a
number of important dissidents evolved a strategy for
survival. In a phrase, they decided to live "as if."

I'm never certain which author can claim the credit
for this mild-sounding but actually deeply subversive
and ironic decision. Vaclav Havel, then working as a
marginal playwright and poet in a society and state that
truly merited the title of Absurd, realised that "resistance" in its original insurgent and militant sense was impossible in the Central Europe of the day. He therefore
proposed living "as if" he were a citizen of a free society,
"as if" lying and cowardice were not mandatory patriotic
duties, "as if" his government had actually signed (which
it actually had) the various treaties and agreements that
enshrine universal human rights. He called this tactic
"The Power of the Powerless" because, even when disagreement can be almost forbidden, a state that insists

on actually compelling assent can be relatively easily made to look stupid. You can't achieve 100 percent control over humans and, if you could, you could not go on doing so. It is—fortunately—too much responsibility for any human to assume, not that this keeps the control freaks from continuing to try.

At around the same time and alarmed in a different way by many of the same things (the morbid relationship of the Cold War to the nuclear arms race), Professor E.P. Thompson, whom I recommended to you earlier, proposed that we live "as if" a free and independent Europe already existed. Some people are still offended if one mentions these two men in the same breath—and Thompson would never have claimed that they both ran the same risks—but actually the two movements for human rights and disarmament were latently symbiotic at the beginning and had become quite closely related by the end. And we know with certainty, from the memoirs of some of the "statesmen" of the period, that it was the stubborn, nonviolent, cultural and political rebellions of those years that impelled them to recast their assumptions. The process often involved an inversion in the usual relationship between the ironic and the literal. The "People Power" moment of 1989, when whole populations brought down their absurd rulers by an exercise of arm-folding and sarcasm, had its origins partly in the Philippines in 1985, when the dictator Marcos called an opportunist "snap election" and the voters decided to take him seriously. They acted "as if" the vote were free and fair, and they made it so. (The forgotten fact that the Soviet ambassador to Manila took the side of Marcos was also a portent of a kind.)

Again, I've slipped into recounting these legendary moments as if they vindicated dissenters, as they most certainly do, and as if they were self-evident "good, brave causes," which they most certainly were. But it's important to remember the many dreary years when the prospect of victory appeared quite unattainable. On every day of those years, the "as if" pose had to be kept up, until its cumulative effect could be felt. Many of the greatest "as if" practitioners—including Thompson himself, and men like Frantisek Kriegel in then Czechoslovakia—did not live long enough to see the grand production for which they had kept up the optimistic but phlegmatic rehearsals.

One could add further examples. In the late Victorian period, Oscar Wilde—master of the pose but not a mere *poseur*—decided to live and act "as if" moral hypocrisy were not regnant. In the Deep South in the early 1960s, Rosa Parks (after some arduous dress rehearsals of her own) decided to act "as if" a hardworking black woman could sit down on a bus at the end of the day's labor. In Moscow in the 1970s, Aleksandr Solzhenitsyn resolved to write "as if" an individual scholar could investigate the history of his own country, and publish his findings. They all, by behaving literally, acted ironically. In each case, as we know now, the authorities were forced first to act crassly and then to look crass, and eventually to fall victim to stern verdicts from posterity. However, this was by no means the guaranteed outcome and there must have been days when the "as if" style was exceedingly hard to keep up.

All I can recommend, therefore (apart from the study of these and other good examples) is that you try to cultivate some of this attitude. In an average day, you may well be confronted with some species of bullying or bigotry, or some ill-phrased appeal to the general will, or some petty abuse of authority. If you have a political loyalty, you may be offered a shady reason for agreeing to a lie or a half-truth that serves some short-term purpose. Everybody devises tactics for getting through such moments; try behaving "as if" they need not be tolerated and are not inevitable.

VI

A postscript to the above: be prepared in advance for the arguments you will hear (even in your own head) against such a mode of conduct. Some of these are very seductive. What difference does it make, you may be asked (or ask yourself). There's no good answer to this question, as it happens. The universe may well be Absurd, and one's life is in any case certain to be a short one. However, this need not mean that we do not reserve the term "absurd" for the self-evidently irrational or unjustifiable. You can't hope to change human nature or Human Nature; true enough again if slightly tautologous, because Nature is a given. But nobody accepts all human behavior or human conduct as unalterable on that basis.

Other invitations to passivity or acquiescence are more sly, some of them making an appeal to modesty. Who are you to be the judge? Who asked you? Anyway, is this the propitious time to be making a stand? Perhaps one should await a more favorable moment? And—aha!—is there some danger of giving ammunition to the enemy?

I have two favorite texts that I keep by me to exorcise these sorts of temptation. One is an essay written by George Orwell in November 1945 and entitled "Through a Glass, Rosily." He was writing at a time when the Red Army had just "liberated" much of Nazi-occupied Europe, and when it was considered very poor form in some circles to make any criticism of the liberators. The Vienna correspondent of *Tribune*, the socialist weekly for which Orwell worked, had however seen fit to mention the rape and looting committed by Soviet forces in the city:

> *The recent article by Tribune's Vienna correspondent provoked a spate of angry letters which, besides calling him a fool and a liar and making other charges of what one might call a routine nature, also carried the very serious implication that he ought to have kept silent even if he knew he was speaking the truth.*
>
> *Whenever A and B are in opposition to one another, anyone who attacks or criticises A is accused of aiding and abetting B. And it is often true, objectively and on a short-term analysis, that he is making things easier for B. Therefore, say the supporters of A, shut up and don't criticise: or at least criticise "constructively," which in practice always means favourably. And from this it is only a short step to arguing that the suppression and distortion of known facts is the highest duty of a journalist.*

Taking an excellent example of the process at work, Orwell cited the cleverness of Nazi propaganda in the war that had just ended:

Among others they broadcast E.M. Forster's A
Passage to India. And so far as I know they didn't
even have to resort to dishonest quotation. Just because
the book was essentially truthful, it could be made to
serve the purposes of Fascist propaganda. According to
Blake,

> *A truth that's told with bad intent*
> *Beats all the lies you can invent*

and anyone who has seen his own statements
coming back at him on the Axis radio will feel the force
of this. Indeed, anyone who has ever written in defense
of unpopular causes or been the witness of events that
are likely to cause controversy, knows the fearful
temptation to distort or suppress the facts, simply
because any honest statement will contain revelations
that can be made use of by unscrupulous opponents. But
what one has to consider are the long-term effects.

One who had anticipated these long-term consequences, but who also cared about the immediate ones,
was F.M. Cornford, a witty Cambridge academic of the
Edwardian period who had become used to every possible High Table euphemism and Senior Common Room
obfuscation. He anatomised them all in his 1908 treatise,
Microcosmographia Academica. The passage I'll give you is
from chapter 7, entitled "Arguments":

There is only one argument for doing something; the
rest are arguments for doing nothing.

43

Since the stone axe fell into disuse at the close of the Neolithic Age, two other arguments of universal application have been added to the rhetorical armoury by the ingenuity of mankind. They are closely akin; and, like the stone axe, they are addressed to the Political Motive. They are called the Wedge and the Dangerous Precedent. Though they are very familiar, the principles, or rules of inaction, involved in them are seldom stated in full. They are as follows:

The Principle of the Wedge is that you should not act justly now for fear of raising expectations that you may act still more justly in the future—expectations that you are afraid you will not have the courage to satisfy. A little reflection will make it evident that the Wedge argument implies the admission that the persons who use it cannot prove that the action is not just. If they could, that would be the sole and sufficient reason for not doing it, and this argument would be superfluous.

The Principle of the Dangerous Precedent is that you should not now do any admittedly right action for fear you, or your equally timid successors, should not have the courage to do right in some future case, which, ex hypothesi, is essentially different, but superficially resembles the present one. Every public action that is not customary, either is wrong, or, if it is right, is a dangerous precedent. It follows that nothing should ever be done for the first time.

Another argument is that "the Time is not Ripe."
*The Principle of Unripe Time is that people should
not do at the present moment what they think right at
that moment, because the moment at which they think
it right has not yet arrived.*

You may, and I assure you of this, be certain that you will meet some combination of these arguments and evasions as you go through life. You may not always have the energy to combat each of them every time; you may find that you want to husband and conserve your resources for a better cause or a more propitious day. Beware of this tendency in yourself. Be alert, especially, for that awful day when—without even having meant to do so—you find that you have uttered one of these consoling and corrupting formulations yourself.

(Here's a case, incidentally, where neither the sacred nor the profane are of any help. I've sometimes found it useful to say, dammit, I have only one life to live and I won't spend a moment of it on some dismal compromise. But then comes the unprompted thought: with only one life span might I not save some time by ducking this one minor combat? I imagine that those who hope for the hereafter are tempted in the same way but in a different idiom; many are the issues of principle that seem trivial *sub specie aeternitatis*.)

VII

I'm so glad that you liked the *Microcosmographia*. It's a delight in itself, of course, but I keep it by me as a reminder that many questions are actually quite simple. There's a small paradox here; the job of supposed intellectuals is to combat oversimplification or reductionism and to say, well, actually, it's more complicated than that. At least, that's part of the job. However, you must have noticed how often certain "complexities" are introduced as a means of obfuscation. Here it becomes necessary to ply with glee the celebrated razor of old Occam, dispose of unnecessary assumptions, and proclaim that, actually, things are *less* complicated than they appear. Very often in my experience, the extraneous or irrelevant complexities are inserted when a matter of elementary justice or principle is at issue.

My best illustration here would be the case of my dear friend Salman Rushdie. You would think, perhaps, that when he was assaulted by a theocratic *fatwah* in 1989, his fellow authors would have rushed to his defense. Here was an open incitement to murder, accompanied by the offer of a bounty and directed at a writer of fiction who wasn't even a citizen of the said theocracy.

But you would have been astonished to see the amount of muttering and hanging back that went on. Had his novel perhaps been "offensive"? Were the feelings of pious Muslims not to be considered? Was he not asking for trouble? Surely he knew what he was doing? and so forth. Several senior Western statesmen, often of the law-and-order and "antiterrorist" school, took refuge in similar evasive formulations.

In public debates with those who worried about the blasphemous or profane element in the novel, or who said that they did, I would always begin by saying, look, let's get one thing out of the way. May I assume that you are opposed without reservation to the suborning of the murder, for pay, of a literary figure? It was educational to see how often this assurance would be withheld, or offered in a qualified form. In those cases, I would refuse to debate any further. So I was a reductionist in that instance, and proud of my simple-mindedness.

Another example, also from experience. In 1968 I travelled to Cuba. The revolution was still young; Che Guevara's murder was a memory only a few months old; the Castroites maintained that their version of socialism would not be modelled on the dreary example of Russia; there was a good deal of play and latitude. I'm not relating this to you by hindsight, because I was then a member of a Marxist group that had strong reservations about "Fidelism" (and if you like, I'll tell you the story of my political formation in another letter). Anyway, discussions and arguments were intense and, in the year of Vietnam and Paris and Prague, seemed to be—and sometimes were—of real moment. I remember particularly a seminar with Santiago Alvarez, the grand old man of Cuban cinema. Film was the special medium of the Cuban revolution and he assured us that it was unfettered. Completely unfettered? Well, he said with a slight laugh, there is one thing that is not done. No satirical portrayal of the Leader will be permitted. (The slight laugh was at the very idea that anyone would even dream of proposing such a thing.) I said, quite simply, that if the main subject of Castro was off-limits then, in effect, there could be no real satire or criticism at all. I had heard and read of the term "counterrevolutionary," but this was the first time I heard it applied in all seriousness—and to myself, at that. Again, I claim no courage for making such an elementary point, and I ran no risk save the obloquy of some of those present. But I can't forget the dead silence as I passed my observation. At another meeting, where we heard many boasts—some of them truthful—about the advances in medical care and literacy, I inquired whether a Cuban citizen could start his own magazine, or travel outside the country and return to it. Again, the view seemed to be that only a narcissist and unsound element would intrude such a question. I've been back to Cuba many times since, to find that these and related questions have become urgent (and their postponement absolutely fatal to the society). Back then, I was only asking about the obvious, and perhaps

We are an adaptable species and this adaptability has enabled us to survive. However, adaptability can also constitute a threat; we may become habituated to certain dangers and fail to recognise them until it's too late. Nuclear armaments are the most conspicuous example; as you read this you are in effect wearing a military uniform and sitting in a very exposed trench. You exist at the whim of people whose power does not derive from your own consent and who regard you as expendable, disposable. You merely failed to notice the moment at which you were conscripted. A "normal" life consists in living as if this most salient of facts was not a fact at all.

I tell myself every day that I do not recognise the legitimacy of a government that puts me in this position. I do not grant even my "elected" leaders the power of life and death over myself, let alone over all present, future and indeed past forms of life, all of which they arrogate the right to extirpate at an instant's notice. Nor was I ever asked if I would grant that power, even supposing for a moment that I had the right to grant it on behalf of others, which I do not for a moment believe that I do.

However, when meeting a minister or senior functionary of this regime, which is a privilege I quite often enjoy, I do not act as if I am shaking Caligula's blood-bolted mitt. (I do sometimes content myself with thinking that if they knew what was in my mind and heart, they would shrivel as if cursed and blasted.) So I practise

VIII

How to ward off atrophy and routine, you ask? Well, I can give you a small and perhaps ridiculous example. Every day, the *New York Times* carries a motto in a box on its front page. "All the News That's Fit to Print," it says. It's been saying it for decades, day in and day out. I imagine that most readers of the canonical sheet have long ceased to notice this bannered and flaunted symbol of its mental furniture. I myself check every day to make sure that the bright, smug, pompous, idiotic claim is still there. Then I check to make sure that it still irritates me. If I can still exclaim, under my breath, *why* do they insult me and *what* do they take me for and what *the hell* is it supposed to mean unless it's as obviously complacent and conceited and censorious as it seems to be, then at least I know that I still have a pulse.

You may wish to choose a more rigorous mental workout but I credit this daily infusion of annoyance with extending my life span.

IX

You seem to have guessed, from some remarks I have already made in passing, that I am not a religious believer. In order to be absolutely honest, I should not leave you with the impression that I am part of the generalised agnosticism of our culture. I am not even an atheist so much as I am an antitheist; I not only maintain that all religions are versions of the same untruth, but I hold that the influence of churches, and the effect of religious belief, is positively harmful. Reviewing the false claims of religion I do not wish, as some sentimental materialists affect to wish, that they were true. I do not envy believers their faith. I am relieved to think that the whole story is a sinister fairy tale; life would be miserable if what the faithful affirmed was actually the case.

Why do I say that? Well, there may be people who wish to live their lives under a cradle-to-grave divine supervision; a permanent surveillance and monitoring. But I cannot imagine anything more horrible or grotesque. It would be worse, in a way, if the supervision was benign. (I have my answer ready if I turn out to be mistaken about this: at the bar of judgement I shall argue that I deserve credit for an honest conviction of unbelief, and must in any case be acquitted of the charge of hypocrisy or sycophancy. If the omnipotent and omniscient one does turn out to be of the loving kind, I would expect this plea to do me more good than any trashy casuistry of the sort popularised by Blaise Pascal. One could also fall back upon the less principled and more shiftily empirical defense offered by Bertrand Russell: "Oh Lord, you did not give us enough evidence.")

I think that this conviction does bear upon the mental and moral resources that are necessary if one hopes to live "as if" one were free. In a much-quoted reflection on America's original sin, Thomas Jefferson said, "I tremble for my country when I remember that god is just." However, if there really was a god, and he really was just, then there would be little enough for believers to tremble about; it would be a consolation that infinitely outweighed any imaginable earthly care.

I have met many brave men and women, morally superior to myself, whose courage in adversity derives from their faith. But whenever they have chosen to speak or write about it, I have found myself appalled by the instant decline of their intellectual and moral standards. They want god on their side and believe they are doing his work—what is this, even at its very best, but an extreme form of solipsism? They proceed from conclusion to evidence; our greatest resource is the mind, and the mind is not well-trained by being taught to assume what has to be proved.

This arrogance and illogic is inseparable even from the meekest and most altruistic religious affirmations. A true believer must believe that he or she is here for a purpose and is an object of real interest to a Supreme Being; he or she must also claim to have at least an inkling of what that Supreme Being desires. I have been called arrogant myself in my time, and hope to earn the title again, but to claim that I am privy to the secrets of the universe and its creator—that's beyond my conceit. I therefore have no choice but to find something suspect even in the humblest believer, let alone in the great law-givers and edict-makers of whose "flock" (and what a revealing word *that* is) they form a part.

Even the most humane and compassionate of the monotheisms and polytheisms are complicit in this quiet and irrational authoritarianism: they proclaim us, in Fulke Greville's unforgettable line, "Created sick—Commanded to be well." And there are totalitarian insinuations to back this up if its appeal should fail. Christians, for example, declare me redeemed by a human sacrifice that occurred thousands of years before I was born. I didn't ask for it, and would willingly have foregone it, but there it is: I'm claimed and saved whether I wish it or not. And if I refuse the unsolicited gift? Well, there are still some vague mutterings about an eternity of torment for my ingratitude. This is somewhat worse than a Big Brother state, because there could be no hope of its eventually passing away.

In any case, I find something repulsive in the idea of vicarious redemption. I would not throw my numberless sins onto a scapegoat and expect them to pass from me; we rightly sneer at the barbaric societies that practice this unpleasantness in its literal form. There's no moral value in the vicarious gesture anyway. As Thomas Paine pointed out, you may if you wish take on another man's debt, or even offer to take his place in prison. That would be self-sacrificing. But you may not assume his actual crimes as if they were your own; for one thing you did not commit them and might have died rather than do so; for another this impossible action would rob him of individual responsibility. So the whole apparatus of absolution and forgiveness strikes me as positively immoral, while the concept of revealed truth degrades the whole concept of the free intelligence by purportedly relieving us of the hard task of working out ethical principles for ourselves.

You can see the same immorality or amorality in the Christian view of guilt and punishment. There are only two texts, both of them extreme and mutually contradictory. The Old Testament injunction is the one to exact an eye for an eye and a tooth for a tooth (it occurs in a passage of perfectly demented detail about the exact rules governing mutual ox-goring; you should look it up in its context). The second is from the Gospels and says that only those without sin should cast the first stone. The first is the moral basis for capital punishment and other barbarities; the second is so relativist and "non judgmental" that it would not allow the prosecution of Charles Manson. Our few notions of justice have had to evolve despite these absurd codes of ultravindictiveness and ultracompassion.

I can speak with more experience of the Christian propaganda, since I was baptised as an Anglican, educated at a Methodist boarding school with compulsory religious instruction (which I enjoyed and which taught me a good deal) and was once received into the Greek Orthodox Church for reasons that are irrelevant here. But I also had a Jewish mother and was once married by a distinguished rabbi (who I suspected of being a secret Einsteinian agnostic). Judaism has some advantages over Christianity in that, for example, it does not proselytise—except among Jews—and it does not make the cretinous mistake of saying that the Messiah has already made his appearance. (When Maimonides says that the Messiah will come but that "he may tarry," we see the origin of every Jewish shrug from Spinoza to Woody Allen.) However, along with Islam and Christianity it does insist that some turgid and contradictory and sometimes evil and mad texts, obviously written by fairly unexceptional humans, are in fact the word of god. I think that the indispensable condition of any intellectual liberty is the realisation that there is no such thing.

X

You write to remind me that many exemplary people have been sustained by their faith. (Actually, if I may be slightly strict with you, you don't remind me of the fact. I was already quite aware of it. And I have read, and read of, Dr. Martin Luther King and Dietrich Bonhoeffer and many of the others whom you mention.) But let me ask you in turn: Are you saying that their religious belief was a sufficient or a necessary condition for their moral actions? In other words, that without such faith they would *not* have opposed racism or Nazism? I think I have a higher opinion of both men than to say that of them. It may have helped them to employ religious rhetoric, and it certainly aided them in gaining a following. (There have always been societies, by the way, in which the pulpit is the only outlet that is granted leeway or relative immunity.) But, as Laplace is supposed to have said when demonstrating his model of the solar system at court, and on being asked where the Prime Mover was: "It can work without that assumption."

You could have gone further and pointed out that some heroic figures like William Lloyd Garrison, the father of Abolitionism, were devout believers. However, this would have involved you in recognising that Garrison's actual theology, concerning the "Covenant with Death" that the Union had made, was of the same branch as is now professed by Ian Paisley (and that it incidentally called for the destruction, not the preservation, of the Union and the Constitution.) We are fortunate, in other words, to be able to salute his example and discard his worldview. I have also met many courageous and selfless rebels who are unreflective devotees of Islam, or unquestioning believers in Communism. These people, in my judgement, do not really deserve the name of dissident or oppositionist, because one can see future oppressions already inscribed in their thought patterns. No one can be entirely sure that any solution he proposes will not contain its own woes and pains by way of unintended consequence. But one must recoil when the evident and probable consequences are in fact intended, and nothing makes this more certain than the promulgation of articles of faith.

Of course, faith can be admirably "simple." And, though I distrust the way in which simple-mindedness is often exalted by the religious, it may also have its appeal. There was an Austrian Catholic farmer named Franz Jagerstatter who refused to be conscripted into the army of the Third Reich. He gave as his reason his maddeningly simplistic belief that he was under higher orders— to love his neighbor as himself. They beheaded him for his impudence. Very well—I doff my hat. (Herr Jagerstatter was under consideration for canonisation when the Vatican was looking urgently for a Holocaust martyr in the 1980s, and having difficulty in coming up with one. However, it turned out that his pastors and confessors had urged him to don the Nazi uniform and obey the law, which spoiled the whole effect.)

Simplicity, however, is too often allied with credulity for my taste. And the credulous, especially en masse, are not a reassuring sight. As the great Eugene Debs used to tell his socialist voters in the 1912 election campaign, he would not lead them into a Promised Land even if he could, because if they were trusting enough to be led in, they would be trusting enough to be led out again. He urged them, in other words, to do their own thinking. Thus I'm not impressed when G.K. Chesterton and other apologists repeat their mantra: "If people cease to believe in God they do not believe in nothing but in anything." It seems to me that the original belief furnishes evidence for both parts of the latter half of the proposition: a willingness to believe both in nothing, because it doesn't exist just because they say so, *and* in anything, because one faith is very likely to be exchanged for another.

I repeat: what really matters about any individual is not what he thinks, but how he thinks. Our conversation has been about the constituents that might go to make up an independent and a questioning person; a dissenter and freethinker. This project cannot best be approached or undertaken in a kneeling or prostrate position. I touched on the threat of hell with which the devout have always reinforced their ostensibly kindly recommendations, but just consider for a moment what their heaven looks like. Endless praise and adoration, limitless abnegation and abjection of self; a celestial North Korea. (Just to spice things up, some religions promise a good deal of carnal bliss and I think I have already mentioned one of the Church fathers, Tertullian, who also dangled the tempting option of viewing the torments of the damned. All this proves is that religion is man-made, and that men have created gods in their own image rather than the other way about. Only a humorless tyrant could want a perpetual chanting of the praises that, one has no choice but to assume, would be of the innate virtues and splendors furnished him by *his* creator, infinite regression, drowned in praise!)

I am not a supporter of materialist individualism in the Ayn Rand style, nor do I yearn for Nietzschean status. However, there *is* something irreducibly servile and masochistic about the religious mentality. And the critical and oppositional stance does ultimately rest on a belief in the capacity and pride of the individual, while religion tends to dissolve this into a sickly form of collectivism (remember "the flock"). Even at its most beautifully expressed this has a coercive undertone; as a matter of fact the bell does *not* always toll for thee, however much you may believe in human solidarity. Religion is, and always has been, a means of control. Some of those who recommend religion—I am thinking of the school of Leo Strauss—are blunt enough to make this point explicit: it may be myth and mumbo-jumbo but it's very useful for keeping order. If you want to be able to live at an angle to the safety and mediocrity of consensus you will do well not to begin by granting one of its first premises.

Sigmund Freud was surely right when he concluded that religious superstition is ineradicable, at least for as long as we fear death and fear the darkness. It belongs to the childhood of our race, and childhood is not always—as Freud also helped us to understand—our most attractive or innocent period. I am almost tempted to argue for the moral superiority of secular humanism; it is at least free from any taint of opportunist wish-thinking. (I do not delight in the thought of my annihilation, and I am not always consoled even by David Hume's stoic reflection that, after all, I was also nothing before I was born.) However, those who persecute religion are to be avoided at all costs. Antigone taught us to trust the instinct that is revolted by desecration. Sublime works of painting and architecture and poetry have been wrought by those who, in my humble opinion, were laboring under a misapprehension (as their religious leaders indirectly confirmed by their own profanities and book-burnings and "crusades" and inquisitions.) What I propose to you is a permanent engagement with those who think they possess what cannot be possessed. Time spent in arguing with the faithful is, oddly enough, almost never wasted. The argument is the origin of all arguments; one must always be striving to deepen and refine it; Marx was right when he stated in 1844 that "the criticism of religion is the premise of all criticism."

"Science," as we call it, or objective and disinterested inquiry as it should be called, has helped contain and domesticate religion and vulgar Creationism but will never succeed in dethroning it. We live in a time when the origins of the cosmos are becoming at least potentially knowable, and when the nature of humanity—its original encoding and its relation to other species—is becoming more and more distinct. Nonetheless, the argument from design still keeps recurring like a jack-in-the-box, even if (or perhaps because) it rests on that combination of tautology and infinite regression. In a way, there's no mystery about this. After all, believing what I believe about the likely randomness of human life, why do I care to write a tract like this one, advocating what I consider to be the glories of Promethean revolt and the pleasures of skeptical inquiry? What's the point? I have no answer to the question, which I believe to be unanswerable, and that is one unassailable reason why I so heartily distrust those who claim that they *do* have an answer. But at least they have the question, and that's something.

I should not even attempt to sermonise, yet I do warn you that if you feel capable of going into "internal exile" and living against the stream, you can expect some dark nights of—all right—the soul. But to undertake this and then to seek external or invisible aid would surely be to miss the point. A degree of solitude and resignation is necessary to begin with. Some people can't bear solitude, let alone the idea that the heavens are empty and that we do not even succeed in troubling their deafness with our bootless cries. To be an exile or outcast on a remote shore—many minds turn away in terror and seek any source of cosiness. I can only say that, not only when it is compared to the ghastliness of Eternal Paternalism, the concept of loneliness and exile and self-sufficiency continually bucks me up. (And one might also, when confronted with this unadorned reality, learn to treat one's fellow exiles with more consideration and respect. But let's not ask for the moon.)

■ XI

Yours is not the only mail that I read, as I'm sure you appreciate, and so I know quite well that I can appear insufferable and annoying. Worse than that, I know that I can appear insufferable and annoying *without intending to do so*. (An old definition of a gentleman: someone who is never rude except on purpose.) I seem to fail this test; a beloved friend once confided to me that my lip—I think he said the upper one—often has a ludicrous and sneering look and my wife added that it takes on this appearance just when I seem least to be aware of it. I freely admit that I was hugely unsettled by these criticisms and observations, and have spent quite some time wondering how long I'd been rude by accident instead of by design. And what of the times when I have felt myself on top form, tossing and goring my opponents, sparkling my way through the repartee, while producing no effect save dull and baffled rage?

Without changing this distressing subject, I am bound to admit that I don't give a damn when similar criticisms come from those who are not friends or lovers. My mailbag and my e-mail often contain praise (why should I conceal the fact?) and even admiration, but when the note is hostile it is usually hostile in a particular key. The words are variously sorted and—all right, I'll allow myself this— very often misused or mis-spelled. But the hiss of the word "elitist" is almost never omitted.

I know why this accusation is supposed to hurt. (I know it partly because I used to employ it myself.) And I have seen people go to enormous lengths to avoid the charge, or to repudiate it. However, it no longer has the power to sting me. Let me explain why. Many honorable rebels and dissenters in the past were acting and speaking, as it were, for the voiceless and the unrepresented. "Elitist" though this may have been—it had one of its culminations in the scheme for a vanguard party that would actually substitute for the masses—it nonetheless sanctified itself by the reference to "the people." Even the preamble to the United States Constitution, which was written by men who held other people as property, opens with the invocation "We the People . . ." In numerous invocations before and since, this tribute paid by vice to virtue has been a strong motif. Even sovereigns who speak of "My People" are making a semiconscious nod to the idea. Which is exactly where the trouble arises.

Because there is an alternative account of dissent, wherein those who try to tell the truth are derided by the crowd, or silenced by public opinion. You may have a favorite example of your own, and if you don't you ought to have one. The case that still moves me the most—moves me even more than Zola—is the story of those civilised and intelligent (and democratic) individuals who opposed the declaration of the First World War. They were right, and they were decent, and they were also prescient. One might relax the term "prescient" in retrospect, because the horrors that eventuated were greater by far than the horrors they had foreseen. But if you consult the record and see what happened to them—Jean Jaures shot down by a fanatic, Karl Liebknecht imprisoned for his principles, Bertrand Russell silenced—you can see the suicide of a civilisation. And, most of the time, the cheery and patriotic mob would have been as content to see them burned alive as it was to jeer at their burning in effigy.

Now, there may well have been a mob majority for war in 1914. We have no way of testing this proposition, but so it appeared. My point, however, is that governments normally suspicious of the franchise decided on this one occasion to take *vox populi* as *vox dei* (superfluous to add that they were supported in this by their respective established churches and detached institutions of higher learning). The enthusiasm of the populace could be directed at the "stuck-up" and the fancy and fastidious types, while the same populace was prostrate before throne and altar. Susan Sontag in her beautiful novel *The Volcano Lover* gives us a word picture of this mentality at work in a previous epoch. The scene is set in Naples during the bloody monarchist pogrom instigated by Admiral Horatio Nelson (another episode they don't tell you about in school). The crowned pretender has unleashed the mob on the eggheads:

> *A hunting crowd, looking for the telltale signs of*
> *Jacobin identity (apart from having something worth*
> *stealing): a soberly dressed man with unpowdered hair;*
> *someone with trousers; someone with spectacles. . . .*
> *For this is something like nature—which, notoriously,*
> *does not act in its own interests or make judicious*
> *discriminations. Even before this energy exhausts itself,*
> *it will doubtless be reined in by the rulers who have*
> *sanctioned it.*

In that period, the manipulation of populism by elitism was rather a hit-or-miss affair. The "Church and King" mobs unleashed by the authorities in Georgian England were—I don't believe I exaggerate—outlets for energy that might otherwise be directed *at* Church and King. Instead, those who could not read were given cakes and ale for making a pyre of copies of *The Rights of Man*. If you read Dickens's depiction of the Gordon Riots in *Barnaby Rudge* you will strike much the same idea. For the party of order, disorder has always had its uses. It is not only reformers and revolutionaries who claim to speak in the name of the "general will."

Much the same can be said about literary and scientific and even medical matters. Books that were once banned or ridiculed or both, from the time of the condemned Socrates to the time of the forbidden *Ulysses*, have had to be saved not by the crowd, but from the crowd. The evidence of our own evolution had to be broken to people very gently, lest they take up some stupid slogan about the Rock of Ages being preferable to the age of rocks. (Care still has to be taken on this point, when dealing with the tenderheaded.) Many are the works of genius now in public libraries that would have been incinerated if a roll of opinion had been called. And, since I appear to you to be fixated on this point anyway, I trust I will lose none of your respect if I remind you once again that the forces of piety have always and everywhere been the sworn enemy of the open mind and the open book. Do not think for a moment that I have exhausted this point!

Nowadays, "public opinion" is more smoothly and easily ventriloquised. I am sure you have had the experience of making up your own mind on a question and then discovering, on the evening news of the same day, that only 23.6 percent of people agree with you. Ought you to be depressed or disconcerted by this alarmingly exact dissection of the collective brain? Only if you believe that a squadron of undertalented but overpaid pseudo-scientists have truly and verifiably arrived at this conclusion. And perhaps—indeed I would argue, in any case—not even then.

I am sure that you are partially armored, as most intelligent people are, against this kind of thing. Everybody knows that the question can be "loaded"; everybody knows that the sample can be "weighted"; everbody knows that the intelligibility of the questions depends upon the commonplace and the regnant assumptions. It's a mark of sophistication to understand these things, and occasionally to announce that one distrusts or suspects them.

However, these reservations don't amount to a serious critique. The first thing to notice, surely, is that these voyages into the ocean of the public mind are chartered and commissioned by wealthy and powerful organisations, who do not waste their money satisfying mere curiosity. The tactics are the same as those of market research; the point is not to interpret the world but to change it. A tendency to favor one product over another is something not to be passively discovered and observed but to be nurtured, encouraged and exploited.

Thus to the consumer the "poll"—a suggestive word, by the way, and derived from the old and retrogressive "head count" tax—may seem like a mirror of existing opinion. But to the one who produces it, the poll is a swift photograph of the raw material to be worked upon. You may have noticed that popular opinion is not always and invariably cited by the elites. Nor is it consistently tested: I don't remember reading the findings of any poll about the tight money policy of the Federal Reserve. Who would pay (a properly sampled poll is quite an expensive business) for such a thing? No, "public opinion" is not usually recycled until it has been treated. Only then are people informed whether or not their own opinion enjoys the certification of being the majority or approved one. Even general elections, which are supposed to involve voting in the active voice rather than the passive one, have been increasingly compromised by passive dress rehearsals: the polls condition the poll.

One must therefore be willing to risk the charge of "elitism" in order to say that the passive participants in this are often dupes, and that those who run the show are often real elitists. People in the mass or the aggregate often have a lower intelligence than their constituent parts. The word "demagogue" would be meaningless if this were not so. A few years ago, I decided in my own mind that the then-president of the United States was even more of a crook and a liar than his most dogmatic ideological opponents had claimed. Some but not all of this question turned on his own "private" morality, which combined the frigid and the sleazy in a rare combination. One day in California, not long after a freshet of disgusting revelations about this president, I heard on my car radio the results of an "instant poll." In the light of the new disclosures, people were invited to say whether they thought their own moral standards were (a) higher than those of the chief executive or (b) about the same as his or (c) lower. Perhaps 20 percent said "higher," and I remember thinking, well, even at my most self-critical I could have managed to say the same. A broad band in the middle reported themselves as no better but no worse; rightly is this the country that gave us the term "nonjudgmental." And then some 20 percent were announced as saying that they thought their own morals were inferior to Clinton's! (By the way, that was this president's name.) My first thought was of the unguessed-at extent of masochism and servility among the electorate. My second thought—which turned out to be accidentally prescient—was of the genius it had taken, in a discussion of the moral fitness of the leader, to turn it into a plebiscite on the morals of his subjects.

From then on, I was never able to utter my view of the man in public or in private without being told that I was out of step with public opinion. But I never met an actual living, breathing individual who had been consulted by a polling organisation, and I never met anyone who regarded himself as morally inferior to the president. Did I ever think I might have been wrong? Yes, sometimes and briefly. But never because of the supposed majority against me.

Now, if I were writing the above lines as a disappointed politician, I might seem like one of those droning megalomaniacs who can't forgive the laziness or the shortsightedness or the hedonism of their electorates. Brecht caught this attitude very well in 1953, when he noticed a Communist leaflet upbraiding the Berliners for their thoughtless uprising against Stalinism, and dryly suggested that perhaps the Party ought to dissolve the people and select another one. One must avoid snobbery and misanthropy. But one must also be unafraid to criticise those who reach for the lowest common denominator, and who sometimes succeed in finding it. This criticism would be effortless if there were no "people" waiting for just such an appeal. Any fool can lampoon a king or a bishop or a billionaire. A trifle more grit is required to face down a mob, or even a studio audience, that has decided it knows what it wants and is entitled to get it. And the fact that kings and bishops and billionaires often have more say than most in forming the appetites and emotions of the crowd is not irrelevant, either.

▪ XII

I admit to a certain wish to have it both ways on the matter of elitism and populism (a wish that is the stronger for being so seldom gratified). But I think I succeeded in avoiding tautology. You remind me, however, to stress again the fact that "dissent" in our time is thought by many people to be somehow a property of the "Left." Several misapprehensions arise from this one misapprehension, and one of them has to do with a reluctance to criticise popular wisdom or popular culture. Let me give you another even more ludicrous example from the world of opinion polling. When President Reagan was discovered to have cancer in his colon, one major newspaper printed a poll in which people were solemnly asked if they thought the cancer would be cured, would recur, or would go into remission. Now, not even the enthusiasts of ultrademocracy would maintain that there could be any popular insight into the state of affairs in Reagan's bottom. (Indeed, a crucial fact in those days was the extent to which authority was able to conceal the president's true physical and mental condition from the public.) But once again there was the illusion or simulacrum of being consulted.

This was a hoax, and those who fall for hoaxes deserve the name of dupes. My dear friend Ian McEwan, in his novel *The Child in Time*, describes a man so demoralised by tragedy and loss that he is reduced to gaping at daytime TV game shows. Seeing his fellow creatures so eager to humiliate and embarrass themselves, he evolves a name for watching the proceedings and calls it "the democrat's pornography." Let us then agree to judge crowds as we would individuals, and to employ no standard of criticism that we would not allow to be directed at ourselves. (In the age of Reagan, by the way, liberals and Democrats were more promiscuous than they have been since in suggesting that "the people" could be or actually were being fooled by a prestidigitator and a smooth PR machine.)

Milton Friedman might be wrong about sweatshops and free-market opportunities, but he was not wrong to state that one man plus a correct opinion outvotes a majority. Pyotr Kropotkin might have been rather a rarefied anarchist but he had a point when he said that if only one man has the truth, that's enough. Science proceeds by the same moral yardstick; a Marie Curie experimenting on herself is exceptional of course, but an individual researcher with a set of properly tested theses or experiments can and sometimes will confound either a set of established experts or an unbelieving crowd. We owe a great deal to the apparent elitists, such as Machiavelli or Houdini, who by studying arcane information and practice and then by making their findings public, contributed to demystification.

One is sometimes asked "by what right" one presumes to offer judgement. *Quo warranto?* is a very old and very justified question. But the right and warrant of an individual critic does not need to be demonstrated in the same way as that of a holder of power. It is in most ways its own justification. That is why so many irritating dissidents have been described by their enemies as "self-appointed." (Once again, you see, the surreptitious suggestion of elitism and arrogance.) "Self-appointed" suits me fine. Nobody asked me to do this and it would not be the same thing I do if they had asked me. I can't be fired any more than I can be promoted. I am happy in the ranks of the self-employed. If I am stupid or on poor form, nobody suffers but me. To the question, Who do you think you are? I can return the calm response: Who wants to know?

One last straddle of my high horse, then (a beast which, as Gore Vidal once said, one must keep tethered conveniently within reach). I offered to tell you in another time and place about my relations with old Karl Marx, and I notice you have not yet taken me up on it. But I've always found it both fascinating and distressing that one of his best-known "sayings" is not one of his sayings at all. He did not say, and more to the point he did not believe, that religion was the opium of the people. What he did say, in his *Contribution to the Critique of Hegel's Philosophy of Right*, was this:

Religious *distress is at the same time the expression of real distress and the* protest *against real distress. Religion is the sign of the oppressed creature, the heart of a heartless world, just as it is the spirit of a spiritless situation. It is the* opium *of the people.*

The abolition of religion as the illusory *happiness of the people is required for their* real *happiness. The demand to give up the illusions about its condition is the* demand to give up a condition that needs illusions. *The criticism of religion is therefore* in embryo the criticism of the vale of woe, *the* halo *of which is religion.*

Criticism has plucked the imaginary flowers from the chain not so that man will wear the chain without any fantasy or consolation but so that he will shake off the chain and cull the living flower.

You will notice the difference between these rather splendidly nuanced sentences and their consistent, unvarying one-sided vulgarisation. They sum up what I most wish to convey to you in our argument about superiority. One must have the nerve to assert that, while people are entitled to their illusions, they are not entitled to a limitless enjoyment of them and they are not entitled to impose them upon others. Allow a friend to believe in a bogus prospectus or a false promise and you cease, after a short while, to be a friend at all. How dare you intervene? As well ask, How dare you not? Are you so sure you know better? Ask yourself this question a thousand times, but if you are sure, have the confidence and dignity to say so. Remember that saying nothing is also a decision, and that the relativists and the "nonjudgmental" have made up their minds just as much, if not as firmly. This is simply another way of reminding you that, if you decide to pass judgements and make criticisms and take forward positions, you both can and should expect a few hearings to convene on yourself. A welcome prospect, I trust. It certainly helps prevent the art and science of disputation from dying out amongst us.

XIII

The question you ask—what to read and whom to study—is one that I receive quite often. It ought to be an easy inquiry to answer. But it isn't, and this is for a series of reasons. The first and most obvious is that you should not look for arguments from authority. You must have noticed that I make liberal use of extracts and quotations, not just to show off my reading but also to lighten my text and make use of those who can express my thoughts better than I am able to. So I am not immune from the weakness against which I am counselling you. I do have some sources of inspiration to which I recur, but it would not always be clear why they have come to mean what they do to me.

Then there is the question of mood. The oppositional and critical mind need not always be one of engagement and principle; it has to deal with a considerable quantity of discouragement and there are days, even years, when Diogenes has much more appeal than Wilde. I can think of two great authors from the great tradition of East European dissent—Czeslaw Milosz and Milan Kundera—who profited greatly from cultivating the uses of pessimism. In *The Captive Mind* Milosz wrote of the Baltic states, which included his ancestral and beloved Lithuania, as if they had been erased as completely by Stalinism as the American Indians had been extirpated by the successive European conquests. In a number of essays, most notably in the introduction to his novel *The Book of Laughter and Forgetting*, Kundera used the same tone of voice to describe the Russification of Czechoslovakia and other nations in what used to be called *MittelEuropa*. He thought of the awful status quo as permanent and irrevocable. As it happens, I was able to differ with both of them—Milosz in person and Kundera in print—and in time everybody lived to see the survival and renaissance of these cultures. But I did not, I hope, misunderstand the essential Stoicism that was present in their work; there were times when the cause seemed hopeless and yet they would not give it up. One way of facing this impossible position was to be as grim as possible and to treat all hopes as illusions. For those facing a long haul and a series of defeats, pessimism can be an ally. (Apart from anything else, as some American Indians have also discovered, the presentation of the bleakest and starkest possible picture can have the paradoxical effect of mobilising the emotions and the intellect.)

I have never myself been in a situation of apparently hopeless oppression, or had to try and recruit the personal courage to resist such a state of affairs. But from observing those who have, I conclude that the moment of near despair is quite often the moment that precedes courage rather than resignation. In a sense, with the back to the wall and no exit but death or acceptance, the options narrow to one. There can even be something liberating in this realisation. "Here I stand, I can do no other." I don't especially recommend Martin Luther—another of those types who resolve the irresoluble by deciding that they have been issued divine orders—but there is a reason why his phrasing is remembered.

Noam Chomsky, a most distinguished intellectual and moral dissident, once wrote that the old motto about "speaking truth to power" is overrated. Power, as he points out, quite probably knows the truth already, and is mainly interested in suppressing or limiting or distorting it. We would therefore do better to try to instruct the powerless. I am not sure that there is a real difference in this distinction. Ruthless and arrogant though power can appear, it is only ever held by mere mammals who excrete and yearn, and who suffer from insomnia and insecurity. These mammals are also necessarily vain in the extreme, and often wish to be liked almost as much as they desire to be feared. Aleksandr Solzhenitsyn, one of the moral titans of our time, decided to write his nation's hidden history and was reviled, imprisoned and deported for his pains. By the summer of 1987, however, the Soviet authorities had decided to cancel the existing history curriculum in state schools and not to resume it until new books could be produced. Solzhenitsyn could, I am convinced, have gone to his grave quite content *without* this vindication, which he never expected. He had already done what he set out to do. Yet "history" determined that he would enlighten not just his readers, but also a significant number of his former jailers. This doesn't make up for the numberless educated Russians who died wretchedly, without being able to touch either an audience or the authorities, but then again—and in a fashion—it does at least help make up for it.

In a very fine and moving poem about history, and what it has done to those who believe in it, Peter Porter wrote:

HISTORY
Freidrich Kutsky, known as 'Mac',
a lawyer's son who worked
with Russian military inteligence
and sent them warning England
wouldn't fight over Czecholsovakia,
was pushed off a grain freighter
in Lake Superiou by an NKVD man
disguised as an elevator mechanic;
Manfred Löwenherz, 'Tom' to their circle
of University Marxist, helped organize
the destruction of the POUM
in Barcelona (Orwell had heard of
but never met him) and was himself
arrested in Moscow three weeks
after Catalonia surrendered: he is
presumed to have died in prison;

Frank Marshall, called 'The Englander'
because of his unlikely name, went
straight to Comintern Headquarters
and survived the show trials of '36
and '37, only to disappear from his flat
on the evening of the Molotov/Ribbentrop
Pact: his name is mentioned often
in the few authentic papers which
survived from Yezhov's office:
The Szymanowski brothers, Andrew
and Jerzy, led a Soviet expedition
to Zemyla and authenticated
the reports of nickel deposits—
both were murdered when their boat
was strafed by an unknown plane
on an expedition in Bering Strait:
the MVD uses more than ice-picks
was said in Moscow in 1940;
lastly Willy Marx, alias Oskar Odin,
'Old Grandad' to the group, jumped
in front of a Viennese tram the day
before the Anschluss, with plans for
Hitler's assassination in his shoes—
no one knows which Party organization
ordered his death. Six middle-class
boys from a racially-mixed Galician
town, three of them Jews, and only
one with a widow at a New England
College. Their story will not be told.

One of the finest moments in our history occurred when Nelson Mandela was visited by the authorities who had kept him in confinement for a quarter of a century. They had been shaken by international condemnation and also by a general rising of the oppressed. The name of Mandela, which was supposed to have been buried by a long and harsh immurement, was on every lip. All right, they nervously said to him, you can go now. You're a free man. His reply was—I am not leaving. You do not have the power to release me, least of all to release me to gratify yourselves. I shall not leave this cell until I hear that everybody else has been released, and that all the laws of the tyranny have been stricken from the books. At that moment, it was clear who held the keys. (Up until that moment, every sort of pseudo-diplomatic compromise had been proposed to allow the racist usurpers to keep at least some part of their spoil, and to save some part of their face.)

One of the great pleasures of my life, and one of the privileges of advancing age, has been that of revisiting people who I first met or knew as political prisoners, or exiles, or refugees. I first met Thabo Mbeki, now the president of South Africa, sitting on the floor at a scruffy radical party in London (actually, *he* wasn't scruffy at all) in the early 1970s. His father was serving a life sentence back home and he was living for two. I first met Kim Dae Jung, now the president of South Korea and a Nobel Laureate for Peace, when he was living in exile in Virginia, under the disapproval of the Reagan administration. He had survived one attempt by the South Korean junta to kill him and another attempt to kidnap him—this for the temerity of coming a close second in an election—and was in the process of deciding to go home and risk his life again. (When he did go, I went with him on his plane and am still proud of the fact that I was with him when he was rearrested.) A Czech exile friend of mine became his country's foreign minister, so did a Zimbabwean with whom I had once helped organise a protest meeting in Oxford. One of the women at that event also became the speaker of the South African parliament a quarter-century later. Adam Michnik, a witty Polish dissident who was running rings around the Stalinist censors when I met him in 1975, now helps edit one of Warsaw's major newspapers. In Greece and Spain and Portugal, all of which were NATO-supported dictatorships while I was growing up, I interviewed men and women in hiding or on the run who subsequently became ministers, party leaders, diplomats, public intellectuals. My Chilean friend Ariel Dorfman, who I first embraced after he read his defiant poems outside the Chilean embassy in Washington, was fourteen years later the guest of honor at a reception, which I also attended, at that same embassy. There's no thrill quite like this, no satisfaction to match it. And I think I can honestly say that none of these comrades has—as so often happened in history—become in their turn a censor, a policeman, a jailer or a demagogue. There is no iron law that proves Simone Weil's famously pessimistic aphorism, which defined *"La Justice"* as *"cette 'fugitive du camp des* ingly negated by sexless plaster saints and representations of angels) puts us on a useful spot. It strongly suggests that anyone could do what the heroes have done. Our current culture, with its stupid emphasis on the "role model," offers as examples the lives of superstars and princesses and other pseudo-ethereal beings whose lives—fortunately, I think—cannot by definition be emulated.

I offer you two anecdotal examples, one of which I have tried myself before various large audiences in America. Ask in mixed company if anyone can name the last American to win the Nobel Prize for Peace. Nobel awards are well-reported here, especially in this category. You will find that nobody can do it. (The answer is Jody Williams, on behalf of the international campaign to ban land mines in 1997.) But see if you can find anyone who doesn't know that Princess Diana once did a photo-op near a minefield. Our standard for these things is subject to its own Gresham's Law: not only does it recognise the bogus but it overlooks and excludes the genuine. (The fish rots from the head in such matters: President Clinton sent his wife to the princess's funeral but did not give the customary presidential call of congratulation to Ms. Williams, who had criticised him in public for withholding his superpower signature from the land mines treaty.)

My friend Peter Schneider, the great novelistic chronicler of Berlin life, once researched and wrote a true story about a wartime episode. It involved the sheltering of those Berlin Jews who had violated the Nazi race laws by marrying Aryans. Some hundreds of these people were saved, in an informal arrangement whereby some thousands of ordinary Berliners provided a bed for the night here, a ration book there. Peter thought that the publication of this account would be well-received; there is always a market for stories about decent Germans. Instead the reaction was a surly one. It took him some time to realise that by describing the brave and generous but low-level and unheroic conduct of so many citizens, he had undermined the moral alibi of many thousands more, whose long-standing excuse for their own inaction had been that, under such terror, no gesture of resistance had been possible. This depressing discovery need not blind us to the true moral, which is that everybody can do something, and that the role of dissident is not, and should not be, a claim of membership in a communion of saints. In other words, the more fallible the mammal, the truer the example. This sometimes cheers me up.

■ XIV

In Joseph Heller's *Catch-22*, which I hope and trust you have read at least once, there is the following exchange between the anti-hero Yossarian and the mind of military authority:

> *Major Danby replied indulgently with a superior smile, "But, Yossarian, what if everyone felt that way?"*
> *"Then I'd certainly be a damned fool to feel any other way, wouldn't I?"*

When I first read that, I was much more at the mercy of schoolmasters and clergymen than I am now, and more in need of defensive ripostes to their dreary objections about "setting a precedent" or "setting an example." Heller cut straight through all that with his absurdly subversive dialectic; of course if the oddballs and doubters were in a majority they wouldn't be oddballs and doubters. And of course, one never has to worry about there being a surplus of such people. Those who need or want to think for themselves will always be a minority; the human race may be inherently individualistic and even narcissistic but in the mass it is quite easy to control. People have a need for reassurance and belonging. This contrast sometimes discovers itself under pressure: consider two classically "dissident" and quite celebrated remarks by Albert Camus and E.M. Forster. Faced with an unjust colonial war in his native Algeria, where the insurgents would detonate random bombs that might as easily kill his aged mama as they might an occupying soldier, Camus observed that if compelled to choose between Justice and his mother, he might well have to pick his mother. While Forster said that, given a choice between betraying his country or betraying his friends, he hoped he would be courageous enough to betray his country. Both of these sayings need their context—Forster wrote at a time when the phrase "King and Country" was a synonym for fatuous jingoism—but you notice that in both instances the resort is not to lone defiance but to another form of loyalty and adherence; in one case family values and in the other the claim of the coterie.

There is an important paradox at work here: of those who are drawn into oppositional activity or mentality it can often be observed that they are rebellious or independent types. Yet the best of them are actuated by concern for others, and for causes and movements larger than themselves. Throughout the late nineteenth century and much of the twentieth, many of the great Promethean individualists were men and women convinced of the rationality and justice of socialism. (I am thinking of moral and intellectual figures of the status of

Antonio Gramsci, Karl Liebknecht, Jean Jaures, Dimitri Tucovic, James Connolly, Eugene Debs and others. If you don't know of their lives and their work, you are the poorer for it.) For most of my life, I considered myself a modest combatant in that cause and I'm phrasing it like that for two reasons, the first of which is that I've been compelled to recognise that its day is quite possibly done. The second reason—more to the immediate point here—is that such an attachment was supposed to teach you to subordinate yourself to the greater good.

This isn't an absolute contradiction by any means. The enemies of socialism never ceased to sneer about its supposed attachment to regimentation and uniformity, whereas its real history is full of great moments when it actually broke open the "barracks" system of factories and slums, places where human actually were treated like machines—to say nothing of its opposition to militarism and imperialism, two other features of the old world which involved regimenting and conscripting people while using them as property, or as subjects in grand experiments. The socialist movement enabled universal suffrage, the imposition of limits upon exploitation, and the independence of colonial and subject populations. Where it succeeded, one can be proud of it. Where it failed—as in the attempt to stop the First World War and later to arrest the growth of fascism—one can honorably regret its failure.

However, everybody knows the other list of names (and dates, and places) which, though it isn't usually put like this, mark the degeneration of the First and Second Internationals into the Third. And some romantics and dogmatists—I can if you like be included in either definition—even know about the relationship of all this to the Fourth. Another book would be needful here; for the present let's say that there's a whole hidden list of distinguished names, from Andreu Nin to Victor Serge to C.L.R. James, representing a lost generation of people whose dissent and resistance was largely conducted within, and even against, the "Left" as it was generally understood. (They don't teach you this in school, either, but the best writing of George Orwell and of Leon Trotsky is only intelligible as a part of this occluded tradition.) And these same people, who would not surrender the principles that attracted them to the struggle in the first place, were obliterated and defamed as mere posturing "individuals" who furthermore dared to oppose themselves to "history." Never mind "history" for now: to the extent that it is a subjective force at all it has dealt very unkindly with their persecutors and executioners. The point to keep in mind is that when it came to it, these heroes had no stronger moral compass than their Dark Age predecessors and were forced to rely as much on their own consciences, if not indeed more, as on any historical materialist canon.

The essential element of historical materialism as applied to ethical and social matters was (and actually still is) this: it demonstrated how much unhappiness and injustice and irrationality was man-made. Once the fog of supposedly god-given conditions had been dispelled, the decision to tolerate such conditions was exactly that—a decision. "The West," at least, has happily never recovered from this discovery; you would be astounded if you looked up the books and commentaries of only a century ago and saw what was taken for granted before the Marxist irruption. Fatalism and piety were the least of it; this was cynicism allied to utilitarianism. Don't let yourself forget it, but try and profit also from the hard experience of those who contested the old conditions and, in a word or phrase, don't allow your thinking to be done for you by any party or faction, however high-minded. Distrust any speaker who talks confidently about "we," or speaks in the name of "us." Distrust yourself if you hear these tones creeping into your own style. The search for security and majority is not always the same as solidarity; it can be another name for consensus and tyranny and tribalism. Never forget that, even if there are "masses" to be invoked, or "the people" to be praised, they and it must by definition be composed of individuals. Stay on good terms with your inner Yossarian.

Several letters ago, I promised you a few words on the name "radical." Again slightly worn with use, it has a fine pedigree; the great Thomas Paine spoke of "laying the axe to the root" and the essence of the radical definition is that it has its roots, so to speak, in the word "root." Paine is an excellent illustration of this in one way; he saw that the root cause of distress in the thirteen colonies was the Hanoverian monarchy and, at a time when most of the future American leadership was still monarchist and in favor of maintaining the British connection, argued strenuously for independence. On the other hand—not my favorite expression, except when used (as it was) as the title of Fay Wray's autobiography—his engagement with the French Revolution taught him the dangers of fanaticism and fanatics and all those who were sure that they possessed the truth, and the right to impose same. In fact, the noblest verdict on Paine is that he wanted the French Revolution to be more temperate and humane, and the American Revolution (by abolishing slavery and being decent to the Indians) to be more thoroughgoing and profound. But in some ways—obscured by his combat with Burke—this makes him more of a conservative figure. He was certainly a lifelong opponent of "big government" and not just in its monarchic and religious forms. Burke, in turn, though identified with the Tory and royal interest, was a very potent advocate for the rights of the American colonies, for the Bengalis robbed and bullied by the East India Company, and for his fellow Irishmen. The image of counterrevolutionaries concealed in the ranks of the revolution is, from numberless purges and show trials, a familiar one to us. But many is the honorable radical and revolutionary who may be found in the camp of the apparent counterrevolution. And the radical conservative is not a contradiction in terms.

When I was young, I was consumed by the opposition to the Vietnam War and still wish that I could claim to have done more to help the movement against it. In my university generation there were many young Americans who agonised about the military draft; I was involved in assisting their resistance and I know for a fact that it is completely slanderous to say that they worried chiefly about the wholeness of their own skins. (Well, almost completely slanderous; one of the young Americans of my cohort was the self-seeking dodger Bill Clinton.) The point about the draft, as it seemed to many, was that it was theoretically universal and thus anyone who avoided or evaded it was in effect condemning someone else to go instead. This consideration operated very powerfully on those who were more fortunately placed, since their opposition to the war was of a piece with their support for the Civil Rights movement and the "War on Poverty." In effect, their consciences had been collectivised by society, though that was not at all the way we would have phrased it at the time. I thought then and I think now that those who resisted, whether by burning their draft cards or going to jail or going into exile, were absolutely right. There is an obligation, if your "own" government is engaged in an unjust and deceitful war, to oppose it and to obstruct it and to take the side of the victims.

However—and I did not appreciate this until rather later—the draft was abolished because of the arguments of some people who weren't even that much opposed to the war. President Nixon set up a commission to examine the subject, on which sat Professor Milton Friedman—

the celebrated author of *Capitalism and Freedom*—and Alan Greenspan, later celebrated in his turn as chairman of the Federal Reserve, but then best-known as an acolyte of the ultralibertarian Ayn Rand. Between them, these two men persuaded the other members of the Commission that the draft was an unconscionable extension of state power, a form of taxation without representation, and a species of (Friedman's term for it) "slavery." So that while I and others were battling in the streets with the red flag and the flag of the NLF, the apostles of the free market were pressing our demands in the inner sanctum. The irony is probably at the expense of both of us: I draw your attention to it because there are still liberals and social-democrats who regard compulsory military conscription as a form of social program, good for the soul and good for levelling and mixing and social engineering.

Thus in order to be a "radical" one must be open to the possibility that one's own core assumptions are misconceived. I have not, since you ask, abandoned all the tenets of the Left. I still find that the materialist conception of history has not been surpassed as a means of analysing matters; I still think that there are opposing class interests; I still think that monopoly capitalism can and should be distinguished from the free market and that it has certain fatal tendencies in both the short and long term. But I have learned a good deal from the libertarian critique of this worldview, and along with this has come a respect for those who upheld that critique when almost all the reigning assumptions were statist.

I mentioned earlier my friend Adam Michnik, the Polish dissident who I met in the mid–1970s. He was not on the political Right, as were so many Polish anti-Communists, and he indeed had Trotskyist friends (which is how I met him) as well as contacts with the more conventional European Left. However, he made a remark which over time was to change my life. The crucial distinction between systems, he said, was no longer ideological. The main political difference was between those who did, and those who did not, think that the citizen could—or should—be "the property of the state." This had a nice echo of Thomas Paine's attack on slavery—"Man has no property in man." And it matched my own rejection of the thermonuclear national-security state, which regards its subjects as disposable. If you want to pursue truly radical conclusions, I'd recommend that you follow the path indicated by Adam's incisive remark. He easily outlived the Leviathan that dwarfed his little group of critics at the time: with effort perhaps we could all be so lucky.

P.S. A note on language. Be even more suspicious than I was just telling you to be, of all those who employ the term "we" or "us" without your permission. This is another form of surreptitious conscription, designed to suggest that "we" are all agreed on "our" interests and identity. Populist authoritarians try to slip it past you; so do some kinds of literary critics ("our sensibilities are engaged . . . ") Always ask who this "we" is; as often as not it's an attempt to smuggle tribalism through the cus-

XV

Well, no, I don't think that the solidarity of belonging is much of a prize. I appreciate that it can bestow some pride, and that it can lead to mutual aid and even brother- and sisterhood, but it has too many suffocating qualities, and many if not most of the benefits can be acquired in other ways.

That's relatively easy for me to say, as you point out. After all, to have been born in England and to be brought up in its educated class is to have acquired certain securities as a kind of birthright. However, as was once so well said: "What do they know of England, who only England know?" This applies, with the relevant alteration, to any country or culture. I want to urge you very strongly to travel as much as you can, and to evolve yourself as an internationalist. It's as important a part of your education as a radical as the reading of any book.

In the years of my upbringing, before I left for America at the age of about thirty, Britain was making the transition from being a homogenous and colonial society to becoming a multicultural and postcolonial one. I came of a naval and military family with a long tradition of service to the empire; my first conscious memory is of crossing the Grand Harbor at Valetta by ferry, at a time when Malta was still a British colony. As I grew older, part of the background noise was supplied by the collapse of British imperial arrangements in the Suez Canal, Cyprus, Aden and Africa; this noise amplified through the growls of resentment I heard from being brought up in and around British naval bases. My grandfather had served in India in the First World War, my father had been posted in British overseas "possessions" as far distant as the coastal enclaves of China, the Cape of Good Hope, and the Falkland Islands. (When I got married in Cyprus in 1981, he revisited the island for the first time since helping to put down a revolt there a half-century earlier.) A regular occurrence was the arrival of mail from our uncles and aunts and cousins in South Africa, who sometimes came to visit and always seemed vaguely "defensive."

I won't say that I was brought up to think or hear anything ugly—my parents were too intelligent to be encumbered by prejudice—but the prevailing attitude to foreigners was of the "watch out for your wallet don't drink the water" style and this attitude was reinforced by the British gutter press as well as by many politicians. When I started travelling in earnest in my twenties, often to countries that had once been British colonies, I took along my socialist convictions but often had to overcome a squeamish or nervous reluctance to go into the bazaar, so to speak. (As recently as 1993, when I set off on a long tour of Africa for my magazine, not one person in Washington failed to wish me luck in "darkest Africa" "the heart of darkness" "the dark continent." As you'll find when you go to Africa, the first thing you notice is the dazzling light.)

In one way, travelling has narrowed my mind. What I have discovered is something very ordinary and unexciting, which is that humans are the same everywhere and that the degree of variation between members of our species is very slight. This is of course an encouraging finding; it helps arm you against news programs back home that show seething or abject masses of either fanatical or torpid people. In another way it is a depressing finding; the sorts of things that make people quarrel and make them stupid are the same everywhere. The two worst things, as one can work out without leaving home, are racism and religion. (When allied, these two approximate to what I imagine fascism must have felt like.) Freud was brilliantly right when he wrote about "the narcissism of the small difference": distinctions that seem trivial to the visitor are the obsessive concern of the local and the provincial minds. You can, if you spend enough time there, learn to guess by instinct who is Protestant and who is Catholic in Belfast or who is Tamil and who is Sinhalese in Sri Lanka. And when you hear the bigots talk about the "other," it's always in the same tones as their colonial bosses used to employ to talk about them. (Dirty, prone to crime, lazy, very untrustworthy with women and—this is especially toxic—inclined to breed rapidly.) In Cyprus, a place I know and love, almost all communication between the two sides is stalled and inhibited by a military occupation and partition. But there are certain areas of Greek-Turkish cooperation that transcend the local apartheid. One is the sewage system in the divided capital city, because sewage knows no boundaries. The other is a regional sickle-cell blood malady called thalassemia, which affects both communities. I was talking one day to a Greek Cypriot physician who was engaged in joint research with Turkish colleagues on this shared disorder. He said to me that it was a funny thing, but if you looked at a blood sample you couldn't tell who was Turkish and who was Greek. I wanted to ask him whether, before he became a medical man, he had thought that the two nationalities were fashioned from discrepant genetic material.

We still inhabit the prehistory of our race, and have not caught up with the immense discoveries about our own nature and about the nature of the universe. The unspooling of the skein of the genome has effectively abolished racism and creationism, and the amazing findings of Hubble and Hawking have allowed us to guess at the origins of the cosmos. But how much more addictive is the familiar old garbage about tribe and nation and faith.

I make a minor specialism out of the study of partition—one of the legacies of the British empire, by the way, though not exclusively to be blamed on it—and I have crossed most of the frontiers that freeze stupidity and hatred in place and time. The Ledra Palace Hotel checkpoint in Nicosia, the Allenby Bridge across the Jordan, the "demilitarised zone" at Panmunjom in Korea (uncrossable still, though I have viewed it from both sides), the Atari border post that cuts the Grand Trunk Road between Amritsar and Lahore and is the only land crossing between India and Pakistan, the "Hill of Shouts" across which divided villagers can communicate on the Golan Heights (which I've also seen from both sides), the checkpoints that sprang up around multicultural Bosnia and threatened to choke it, the "customs" post separating Gaza from the road to Jerusalem . . . I've stood in the sun or the rain and been searched or asked for bribes by surly guards or watched pathetic supplicants be humiliated at all of these. Some other barriers, like Checkpoint Charlie in Berlin or the British army's bunker between Derry and Donegal or the frontier separating Hong Kong and Macao from China have collapsed or partly evaporated and are just marks in my passport. The other ones will all collapse or dissolve one day, too. But the waste of life and energy that has been involved in maintaining them, and the sheer baseness of the resulting mentality. . . . In some ways I feel sorry for racists and for religious fanatics, because they so much miss the point of being human, and deserve a sort of pity. But then I harden my heart, and decide to hate them all the more, because of the misery they inflict and because of the contemptible excuses they advance for doing so. It especially annoys me when racists are accused of "discrimination." The ability to 'white,'" I was once told—by an African-American clerk, I might add. I explained that white was not even a color, let alone a race. I also drew his attention to the perjury provision that obliged me to state only the truth. "Put 'Caucasian,'" I was told on another occasion. I said that I had no connection with the Caucasus and no belief in the outmoded ethnology that had produced the category. So it went on until one year there was no race space on the form. I'd like to claim credit for this, though I probably can't. I offer you the story, also, as part of my recommendation that one acts bloody-minded as often as the odds are favorable and even sometimes when they are not: it's good exercise.

I don't seem to have said enough about the compensating or positive element of exposure to travel. Just as you discover that stupidity and cruelty are the same everywhere, you find that the essential elements of humanism are the same everywhere, too. Punjabis in Amritsar and Lahore are equally welcoming and open-minded, even though partition means the amputation of Punjab as well as of the subcontinent. There are a heartening number of atheists and agnostics in the six counties of Northern Ireland, even though Ulster as well as Ireland has been divided. Most important of all, the instinct for justice and for liberty is just as much "innate" in us as are the promptings of tribalism and sexual xenophobia and superstition. People know when they are being lied to, they know when their rulers are absurd, they know they do not love their chains; every time a Bastille falls one is always pleasantly surprised by how many sane and decent people were there all along. There's an old argument about whether full bellies or empty bellies lead to contentment or revolt: it's an argument not worth having. The crucial organ is the mind, not the gut. People assert themselves out of an unquenchable sense of dignity.

I have a Somali friend who, during the Western intervention in her unhappy country in 1992, became a sort of clearinghouse for information on human rights. At one point, a group of Belgian soldiers lost their heads and fired into a Somali crowd, killing a number of civilians. At once, Rakiya's switchboard lit up, with every Belgian news desk calling her at once. Alas, these correspondents and editors only wished to know one thing. Were the Belgian soldiers Flemish or Walloon? To this paltry inquiry she replied—I suspect not without relish—that her organisation took no position on tribal rivalries in Belgium. This recollection reminds me that I owe you a letter on the importance of humor.

PS: Since this often seems to come up in discussions of the radical style, I'll mention one other gleaning from my voyages. Beware of identity politics. I'll rephrase that: have nothing to do with identity politics. I remember very well the first time I heard the saying "The Personal Is Political." It began as a sort of reaction to the defeats and downturns that followed 1968: a consolation prize, as you might say, for people who had missed that year. I knew in my bones that a truly Bad

Idea had entered the discourse. Nor was I wrong. People began to stand up at meetings and orate about how they *felt*, not about what or how they thought, and about who they were rather than what (if anything) they had done or stood for. It became the replication in even less interesting form of the narcissism of the small difference, because each identity group begat its subgroups and "specificities." This tendency has often been satirised—the overweight caucus of the Cherokee transgender disabled lesbian faction demands a hearing on its needs—but never satirised enough. You have to have seen it really happen. From a way of being radical it very swiftly became a way of being reactionary; the Clarence Thomas hearings demonstrated this to all but the most dense and boring and selfish, but then, it was the dense and boring and selfish who had always seen identity politics as their big chance.

Anyway, what you swiftly realise if you peek over the wall of your own immediate neighborhood or environment, and travel beyond it, is, first, that we have a huge surplus of people who wouldn't change anything about the way they were born, or the group they were born into, but second that "humanity" (and the idea of change) is best represented by those who have the wit not to think, or should I say feel, in this way.

XVI

Very well, I did promise to take my life in my hands and write about humor. Start with the word "wit," which, as I used it above, means native intelligence or savvy. When we say that someone lives by his wits, we don't mean that he makes an income from stand-up comedy, and when we call someone a half-wit we don't suggest that that person lacks a funny side. But there is a relationship between intelligence and humor and, though it's very unwise to try and describe it, this is what I propose to attempt now.

A good place to start is with my friend Martin Amis, whose whole work is a vivid, lasting illustration of comic brilliance allied to high intelligence. In his memoir *Experience* he revenges himself upon some dolt or other, describing him as humorless and adding that by calling him humorless he means very deliberately to impugn his sense of seriousness. Radicalism is humanism or it is nothing; the proper study of mankind is man and the ability to laugh is one of the faculties that defines the human and distinguishes the species from other animals. (With the other higher mammals, which I do not in the least wish to insult, there may be high levels of

playfulness and even some practical jokes, but no irony.)
An individual deficient in the sense of humor represents
more of a challenge to our idea of the human than a
person of subnormal intelligence; we fear the psycho-
pathic and the reptilian when we meet characters like
Anthony Powell's Widmerpool.

Laughter can be the most unpleasant sound; it's an essential element in mob conduct and is part of the background noise of taunting and jeering at lynchings and ex-
ecutions. Very often, crowds or audiences will laugh
complicitly or slavishly, just to show they "see" the joke
and are all together. (The worst case here is the unfunny
racist joke, requiring the least effort to trigger a laugh response. But there are also consensus comedies so awful
that they require the post-Pavlovian imposition of a
dubbed-in "laugh track.") It's therefore not true to say, as
some optimists do, that humor is essentially subversive. It
can be an appeal to the familiar and the clichéd, a source
of reassurance through shared hilarity. The *Reader's Di-
gest* used to run—perhaps still does run—an excruciating
monthly feature with the writhe-making heading:
"Laughter—The Best Medicine."

That would make it reactionary almost by definition
because the sophisticated element in humor is exactly its
capacity to shock, or to surprise, or to occur unintention-
ally. Freud thought this was worthy of study in his *Wit and
Its Relation to the Unconscious* and in his dream works; the
husband who announces to his wife: "If one of us dies, I'm
moving to Paris." It is told of Freud that when he was

trapped in Vienna by the *Anschluss*, he asked the Nazis for a safe-conduct to leave. They granted this on condition that he signed a statement saying that he had been well-treated. He asked for permission to add an extra sentence and to their delighted surprise wrote: "I can thoroughly recommend the Gestapo to anybody." Professor Frederic Crews assures me, alas, that this never happened.

Had it done so, however, it would have formed part of the record of humor as a resource against the stony, unsmiling face of repressive authority, to say nothing of implacable fate. Everyone has their best example of jokes mocking the old regimes of Eastern Europe; Milan Kundera wrote a whole novel called The Joke about the trouble that could ensue from making the wrong crack at the wrong time and then—arguably the worst part—having to explain or justify it. I have even heard some good bitter jokes from the early stages of the Hitler and Stalin nightmares, though there isn't any Shoah or Gulag humor as such. There is, however, a humor based on ironic Jewish fatalism that goes back through millennia of shrugging and can be traced, as I mentioned in another context, from the exaggerated care with which Maimonides says that, though the Messiah is to be expected, he may tarry. Irony, says Czeslaw Milosz in his poem Not This Way, is "the glory of slaves": the sharp aside and the witty nuance are the consolation of the losers and are the one thing that pomp and power can do nothing about. The literal mind is baffled by the ironic one, demanding explanations that only intensify the

The difficulty with all this, from the radical standpoint, is as follows. Humor is easily enough definable as a weapon of criticism and subversion, but it is very often a mere comfort or survival technique. Ancient authorities understood this well, providing feasts of misrule to entertain the vassals and laying on licensed jesters and fools into the bargain. I have always thought that it must be this that impelled Nietzsche to define a joke as an epitaph on a feeling; the feeling has hardly arisen when it is dissolved or dissipated in a burst of mirth or bathos. An unforgettable moment in *Doctor Zhivago* puts the cynic Komarovsky in the saddle: a salon of bourgeois riffraff falls silent and uneasy as the crowd of workers sings the revolutionary anthem underneath the balcony; he punctures the tension by exclaiming, "Perhaps they'll learn to sing in tune after the revolution!"

It's often said that radicals are humorless; this is certainly not intended as a compliment to the seriousness that they must affect. How wounding is the charge, or how wounding ought it to be? There are not many jokes in Zola, who actually relied more on sarcasm for some of his effects. Nor is the work of George Orwell very rib-tickling, though he could be witty enough at his own expense. (By the way, what is often really meant by the supposed humorlessness of their radicals is their supposed inability to laugh at themselves. But why should they accept an invitation to consider their grand schemes absurd?) Marx was often very funny; I don't know of any Gramsci or Luxemburg gags; at the nadir of the Left in

1915, when he was trying to convene the few remaining delegates for a much-persecuted antiwar conference at Zimmerwald, Trotsky found time to observe that you could now get all of the internationalists in Europe into three stagecoaches.

I'm a partisan of the pro-wit radical faction myself, and that's why I so much admire Oscar Wilde (who was heading for exile and death in France at about the time that Zola was crossing the Channel in the other direction to escape his own persecutors). But I have to admit that this faces us with an apparent paradox of a kind that even Wilde might have found unyielding. The paradox is phrased most tautly by Jean-Paul Sartre in his essay on Baudelaire. (Yes, Sartre, not usually considered natural comic material until the Monty Python team decided to concentrate on the lighter side of *L'Etre et Le Nèant*.) Sartre distinguished between rebels and revolutionaries. The rebel, he says, secretly quite wants the world and the system to remain as it is. Its permanence, after all, is the guarantee of his continuing ability to "rebel." The revolutionary, in contrast, really wishes to overthrow and replace existing conditions. The second enterprise is obviously no laughing matter. As I write this, I realise that I am glad that there were no late-night comedians during the Dreyfus affair. There are times when one wants to hold society's feet to the fire, and to force a confrontation, and to avoid the blandishments of those who always call upon everyone to "lighten up" and change the subject. I think that many great and stern radicals did not *lack* a sense of humor—as the Royalist faction liked to say of the Cromwellian Parliamentarians for example—so much as they felt themselves obliged to be serious. (After all, Cromwell did tell his Puritan fighters to put their faith in god and keep their powder dry, which is also wryness of a kind.) And Tom Lehrer stopped singing when Henry Kissinger won the Nobel Peace Prize, on the grounds that "satire is dead." He was witty enough to know when to keep quiet, which many comedians are not.

Since I am on both sides of this crucial issue, I may as well stay where I am. Humor ought to be pointed—ought to preserve its relationship to wit—and it ought to be fearless. The easiest forms it takes are those of caricature (the clever politician already knows enough to make an offer for the original cartoon, as a show of his goodheartedness and tolerance) and associated forms of mimicry. The mordant forms it takes are the ironic and the obscene. Probably only the latter two forms can be revolutionary. Some dirtbag politician or time-server will not in fact try to buy the original of a cartoon that shows him in the very act of treating his female staff as if they were campaign donations, which is why such truthful cartoons never in fact appear. Nor will a king join in the joke if he is represented as flailing impotently in a four-poster bed, or shown crouching and fuming grimly on a lavatory throne. The great caricaturists of the past were prepared to shock people beyond reason in showing the simple fact that our masters are made from the same damp clay as we are: that's why they (the caricaturists, that is, like Daumier) often went to jail. A rule of thumb with humor; if you worry that you might be going too far, you have already not gone far enough. If everybody laughs, you have failed.

As for the ironic, I shan't attempt a definition here. It's the gin in the Campari, the x-factor, the knight's move on the chessboard, the cat's purr, the knot in the carpet. Its elusive and allusive nature is what makes it impossible to repress or capture. It has a relationship to the unintended consequence. One of its delights is that it can be deployed literally. Voltaire, for example, solemnly added up all the claimed splinters and fragments of the True Cross, as they were displayed in the reliquaries of Christendom, and deduced carefully that the man who had once hung from such an immense artifact must have been a giant. His impiety only "worked" because it took faith at face value.

Since irony is always ready to jog the elbow and spoil the plan of anyone engaged in a high task, and since, if it can be detected at work anywhere, its fingerprints can be found on history, it will have its say most firmly but delicately with anyone claiming to have "history" on his or her side. Bear this ever and always in mind when you hear the tuneful heralds of any grand new epoch. Meanwhile, it could be worth bearing in mind that, if you really care about a serious cause or a deep subject, you may have to be prepared to be boring about it.

the charges against him. It was quite obvious that, were it not for a tight primary race in New Hampshire that spring, he would have got either a stay of execution or even a commutation of sentence. I wrote a column or two about this piece of cold-blooded savagery, and hoped for a response. But it became clear that the usual bleeding-heart liberal types were going to keep silent about this atrocity, because they thought they had found a candidate for the presidency who would suit their needs. So I decided to become a bore. I would insist on mentioning the case whenever I wrote about the governor (who did succeed in becoming president, and who didn't disappoint me) and I banged on about it whenever I was interviewed on radio and TV, or whenever I was asked for my views by a correspondent of any overseas news organisation. My pledge to myself was that I would make the forgotten Mr. Rector as famous as if he'd been executed by a typical law-and-order Republican. Of course I missed that mark—if he'd been executed by a vote-grubbing Right-winger he would have been world-famous right away—but over the course of eight years I did find that people began to react as if they had heard the story. Indeed, I was sometimes greeted with "Oh, not that again," or "You seem obsessed by this" or—my favorite—"Can't we move on?" However, tedium is its own reward and in the year 2000, taking part in a TV panel on the elections, I mentioned George Bush's awful toll of lethal injections in Texas. The chairman, who barely knew me and who had no politics, broke in to say:

"But how is that worse than Clinton executing that crippled black man, Mr. Rector?" He spoke as TV people do, as if everyone would get his point. My mouth did spring open but I'm glad to say that—remembering the admonition about the gift-horse—I had the presence of mind to close it again.

So I entreat you; have no fear of being thought a monomaniac. (If you catch yourself being one, that may be different). It is one of those indicative insults that betrays the prickings of a poor conscience on the other side, or among those who have been easy on themselves. It should be a spur to further droning on your part.

My battle-hardened father, who to his credit tried—even as he failed—to avoid reminiscing too much about the war, once told me that warfare consisted of long periods of tedium punctuated by brief moments of terror. I've since heard this confirmed by many veterans and, in the few war zones I've briefly visited, had the chance to discover its truth for myself. Much depends, therefore, on how one handles the tedious part. The life of a radical is not dissimilar; barricades and Bastilles are not everyday occurrences. It's important to be able to recognise and seize crux moments when they do appear, but much of the time one is faced with quotidien tasks and routines. There's an art and a science to these things; the art consists in trying to improvise more inventive means of breaking a silence, and the science consists in trying to make the periods of silence bearable. Few things, for example, are more forbidding than the elementary civic duty of taking up the case of the wrongfully imprisoned. Visits to the jail, writing letters to indifferent elected officials, meeting with demoralised or paranoid relatives, sessions with lawyers . . . the Dreyfus moment almost never comes. A lot of class warfare can be the same way, keeping up the spirits of the strikers who have no savings, looking up dismal and complex records to find out where the corporation has hidden its money, trying to interest a reporter in telling the story honestly. In the case of some ground-down or ethnically cleansed faraway country, explaining to uncaring people where it is on the map and why it might either matter to them or be, in some way they may not wish to hear, their own responsibility. I don't mean to make any of this appear to be soul-destroying; it will only seem like that if you hope for instant results. The great reward, if that's the right word, lies in the people you will meet when engaged in the same work, the lessons you will learn, and the confidence you will acquire from having some experiences and *convictions* of your own—to set against the received or thirdhand opinions of so many others.

XVIII

Dante was a sectarian and a mystic but he was right to reserve one of the fieriest corners of his inferno for those who, in a time of moral crisis, try to stay neutral. So, since you ask me to go on less like a whiskered veteran and say a bit more about the art than the science, I shall try and be obliging. Again, I'm going to mention some examples from my own limited experience. I always feel slightly self-conscious about doing this, but at least the stories are firsthand and I have noticed myself that, when reading the work of other authors, I never resent the autobiographical. So I shall pretend that I am a stranger to all forms of modesty, including the false.

I have been arrested a few times in various countries, and roughed up a few times as well, and once spent a brief time in jail in Prague during the dying days of the Stalinist regime. I have also heard the occasional shot fired in anger. But most of this was, if I'm to be frank, the result of pretty minor and marginal engagements in which I chose to involve myself. (I once made a speech at a street rally against an apartheid-era South African cricket team, which led the British police to grab and hold me on a charge of incitement to riot. I remember distinctly being disappointed as well as relieved when that charge was dropped; there had been something flattering in this tribute to my rhetorical skill. So you see—I've done mainly summer soldiering.)

The war in Bosnia-Herzegovina in the early 1990s changed all that for me and for many other people I knew. It might sound provincial and (oh dear) *Eurocentric* to say this, but not even those of us who had taken the gloomiest view of the arms race and the Cold War had ever expected to see a full-dress reprise, in Europe, of internment camps, the mass murder of civilians, the reinstitution of torture and rape and deportation as acts of policy. This was the sort of thing we had read about from six decades before; some of us (including myself) had met and got to know some survivors of that period. And of course, in a recess of our minds we had played the imaginary game: what would I do about the knock on the door; how would I react if the neighbors were being marched off to the station?

That tired analogy turned out to be uncomfortably useful, because when all this ghastliness did get under way again, the political class in Europe and America behaved for the most part with the same wretched combination of complacency and complicity that it had exhibited when Fascism first came to call. I haven't got the space to tell the full story here, but I'll do some polemical itemisation of the main headings:

1. In the twentieth century, which was forced to invent the word "genocide," the Ottoman Turks had exterminated the Christian Armenians and the Nazi Germans had tried to eliminate all the Jews. Both outrages took place under the cover of a wider war, and in occupied or disputed territories where there were few independent witnesses. The attempt to destroy the Muslims of Bosnia took place in broad daylight, and was captured on film, and was the cause of the war and not a vile subtext of it.

2. Bosnia had a Muslim plurality but had long been a multicultural polity; many Muslims were themselves secular; the capital city of Sarajevo was a place of mingling and synthesis where large communities of Serbs, Croats, Jews and Bosniaks did rather more than merely coexist.

3. Unlike Serbia and Croatia, the two main contending parties in the Balkan wars, Bosnia did not have, and never has had, any claims on anyone else's territory. The assault on Bosnia, and the brutish siege of Mostar as well as Sarajevo, was concocted in advance by an agreement between two ostensible rivals: the nostalgic fascist Mr. Tudjman and the born-again "national socialist" Mr. Milosevic. This mini Hitler-Stalin pact was known about by NATO, and can be confirmed in the records kept by the participants.

4. Since the aggression against Bosnia openly involved a declared wish for territory and a declared distaste for the existing inhabitants, it very quickly disclosed itself as a war of massacre; we want the land and not the people. Always look to the language: the term "cleansing" was bluntly employed on Belgrade TV to describe the process of emptying and ruining the flourishing towns along the River Drina. And always look to the aesthetic also: most of the destruction and desecration of Bosnia's mosques and cemeteries and cultural sites took place during "cease-fires," as part of a planned erasure that scorned the disguise of "collateral damage."

5. Serbian and Croatian irredentists and cleansers openly fought under the banners of their respective Christian Orthodox and Roman Catholic faiths, and were often blessed by priests and prelates. The Bosnians resisted for the most part as Bosnians; the upshot was that they were invariably described as "the Muslims" whereas no broadcast ever reported that "today, Catholic forces destroyed the bridge at Mostar" or "Orthodox bombardment set fire to the national library of Bosnia in Sarajevo."

6. Given the uneven way that borders and populations actually intersect, in Europe and the Balkans and the Caucasus, it would be suicidal to

allow the forcible triumph of a demagogic and dictatorial regime, which sought to impose the tyrannical notion of congruence between "race" and "state." This would negate the whole idea of Europe, not to say civilisation, and could only lead to more war and further despotism.

This was obvious to me in 1992 and seems even more plain today.

What to do about all this? Bosnia, which had an elected government but not much of an army, and which rotated its vice presidency between Muslims, Croats and Serbs, asked for international protection and, failing that, for a recognition of its right to self-defense. Both proposals were rejected, under the terms of a hypocritical "arms embargo" that ignored the seizure by Serbia of the arsenal of the former Yugoslav National Army. (In rather the same way, the international powers had refused to arm the Spanish Republic, leaving it defenseless against Hitler and Mussolini and, not incidentally, forcing it to turn to Stalin's fraternal and asphyxiating embrace.)

So, like a number of other people, I decided to send myself to Sarajevo. I did this in the full awareness that I might present a ridiculous figure. I did it in the full consciousness that vicarious participation in such events has a slightly sinister as well as a slightly farcical past. But when I examined all this, and a few other things too, I realised that I had no excuse *not* to go. If I could be of no help, that would become evident. If I was making myself absurd or getting in the way, I could count on certain people to tell me. In the result, it's the moment in my life of which I'm the most proud.

I have written about this as much as I can elsewhere, and won't inflict the whole narrative upon you. (However, you should get and read Joe Sacco's cartoon-history *Safe Area Gorazde*, to which I was honored to contribute an introduction. Mr. Sacco's pictorial style as a moral draftsman and mordant observer will be famous one day; of that I can absolutely assure you. New forms of the artistic register are one of the infallible signs of an authentic moment.)

In Sarajevo, which was being bombed and shelled around the clock—and which I had to reach by hitching a ride on a Luftwaffe humanitarian flight, glad that I'd never have to explain this to my late father—I saw people at their best, being maltreated by people at their worst. The population was stubbornly refusing to let the chauvinists be its teachers; insulted and bullied in the name of ethnicity and religion, it simply refused to reply in kind. The deputy commander of the Bosnian armed forces, a gallant soldier named General Jovan Divjak, was a Serb. I interviewed him under fire. The assistant editor of the main daily paper *Oslobodjenjei* ("Liberation") was a Serb named Gordana Knesevic: I became a fund-raiser for this courageous daily after its buildings were razed by deliberate bombardment; it never missed an edition. I also became friendly with its Muslim editor, a man who hated racism and tribalism with a real passion.

I understood "going in," as they say, to beware of overidealising the Bosnians, and to suspect the Utopian tourist in myself and others. The model text here is Orwell's *Homage to Catalonia*; it was surprising, and confirming, to find how often it came up in discussions. Bosnian official propaganda took an internationalist tone; it described Milosevic's army and auxiliary death squads as "Chetniks"—an old antifascist term—rather than as "Serbs." "Death to Fascism"—not a bad slogan—was inscribed on posters everywhere. I still have, framed on my wall, a modest poster that was too intricate for wall-poster display and that I found in a government office that was hit by a mortar shell a few moments after I left it. *Gens Una Summus* ("We are one people") was the superscription. Beneath was a design that incorporated the Catholic and Orthodox crucifixes, the Star of David and the Star and Crescent. Just for once, I thought, it's OK to represent diverse peoples by religious symbols.

There were a few gaunt and sectarian and fundamentalist types on the scene, and there were some gangsterism and corruption too, but these things were debated openly and much criticised, and were thought of as letting down the cause rather than exemplifying it. More important still, in a way, was the fact that Serbian and Croatian oppositionists and democrats, half-stifled by a miasma of superstition and xenophobia in their "own" societies, looked on the defense of Bosnia as a survival issue for their own cause as well.

I still become incensed when I remember the arguments of those who thought that it didn't matter. The British Foreign Office and the French presidency, and the emerging Czars of the Yeltsin regime, all wanted to placate the insane, wicked scheme of "Greater Serbia." I say placate because the term "appease" has become worn out by repetition. A preponderance of the American establishment felt the same way. And so did a large element of the official "Left," whether because it was nostalgic for Tito's Yugoslavia or whether because—this was the American case—it had a conditioned response to anything that might trigger "intervention." All the tired official rhetoric of so many years of deterrence and vigilance, all the propaganda about "Never Again," and all the half-baked themes of isolationism seemed to merge into one stream of euphemism and evasion and hypocrisy. It culminated, as you may remember, with some 10,000 men and boys being butchered after the surrender of Srebrenica, while superpower satellites recorded the proceedings from overhead and while the commander in chief of the pogromists was being received by Western and Russian diplomacy as a "partner in peace." I found that I could not eat enough to vomit enough.

I dwell on this memory for two reasons that bear on our relationship. First, you may have to be pompous as well as boring. I thought then and I think now that the defense of Bosnia-Herzegovina was a civilisation question; that if we had let Bosnia and its culture and civilisation be obliterated we would stand exposed as hollow brought together the best of the Sixty-Eighters and the Eighty-Niners, and showed that there had always been a potential symbiosis of the two. In Sarajevo and Mostar and Tuzla and Zagreb and Dubrovnik, I repeatedly met, without any arrangement to do so, just the people I remembered, and I might have hoped to encounter, from earlier battles. I mustn't idealise this either (if only because there were some notable absentees) but writers and militants who had for years been gesticulating at each other across the petrified frontiers of Old Europe, hoping to kindle an argument and a dialogue, and who had been eloquent against bloc politics and wooden language and the pulverising fear of nuclear extinction, heard the signals from Sarajevo. They helped a worthwhile society to outlive the Hitler-Stalin pact between Tudjman and Milosevic, and to outlive Tudjman and Milosevic themselves. The owl of Minerva, says Hegel, takes wing only at dusk. He meant by this that a historical era can only be evaluated as it draws to a close. In bloody Bosnia I realised that all the disparate and random struggles in which some of us had participated earlier could be made, by this recognition of a hinge or crux moment, to make more than retrospective sense. The next phase or epoch is already discernible; it is the fight to extend the concept of universal human rights, and to match the "globalisation" of production by the globalisation of a common standard for justice and ethics. That may sound mild to the point of the herbivorous: I can assure you it will not be in the least a moderate undertaking. It will provide more than enough scope for the most ambitious radical.

It was touch-and-go for a while in Bosnia; a damned near-run thing, but eventually the force of example was enough to get even the United Nations and the grand diplomacy of the old chancelleries wheezing and clanking into action also. That intervention brought problems of its own and cynicism of its own, but as William Morris put it so finely in *The Dream of John Ball*:

> *Men fight and lose the battle, and the thing that they fought for comes about in spite of defeat, and when it comes it turns out not to be what they meant, and other men have to fight for what they meant under another name.*

That is as "dialectical" as anything in Hegel or Marx, and as ironic as anything in George Eliot. (Incidentally, this is not a primer or a reading list but the work of William Morris and his circle on social and aesthetic questions, is one of the most heroic and beautiful chapters in the history of radicalism, and will repay your study many times over. It is Utopian in the most generous sense of the word.)

My old mentor and friend Robert Conquest, another single-handed historian and truth-teller who has put us all in his debt, is still I think mistaken when he suggests that most of our woes derive from idealists, social engineers and Utopians. He is correct in his way, and we shall never again be able to look indulgently on the sort of radical who claims to act like a pitiless surgeon or a ruthless engineer. However, as often as not you will find that—whatever the high-sounding pretext may be—the worst crimes are still committed in the name of the old traditional rubbish: of loyalty to nation or "order" or leadership or tribe or faith. To train the condemnation upon the Utopians is to miss the historical point (the point made in *Animal Farm*, among other places) that Utopians become tyrants when they start to emulate their former masters. It is also to miss the teleological point that we are somehow so constituted as to feel the permanent lash of discontent; it is not possible to immunise people against the hope of extraordinary change. (Soviet pyscho-surgeons, as Conquest well knows, would place dissidents in mental wards and medicate them forcibly for "reformist delusion": thus the only sane people in society were classified as deranged and antisocial; this practice was not the work of wide-eyed or passionate Utopians.)

The high ambition, therefore, seems to me to be this: That one should strive to combine the maximum of impatience with the maximum of skepticism, the maximum of hatred of injustice and irrationality with the maximum of ironic self-criticism. This would mean really deciding to learn from history rather than invoking or sloganising it.

ENVOI

In his haunting little book *Minima Moralia*, Theodor Adorno wrote that an artistically satisfying film could doubless be made, meeting all the conditions and limitations imposed by the Hays Office (the Hollywood censor of the day), *but only as long as there was no Hays Office*. I have always taken that brilliantly gnomic observation to imply the following two things: First, virtue and merit can become their opposites if they are exacted or compelled. Second, no self-description or definition can be relied upon. (An official of the Teamsters' Union, asked by a Senate hearing if his union was really powerful, responded guardedly but elegantly by saying that being powerful was a little like being ladylike: "If you have to *say* you are, you prob'ly ain't.")

I have not, throughout our correspondence, been quite able to shake off a slight sense of imposture. If you define me as an authority on the radical you may be under an illusion; if I take your invitation at face value I may be making a fool of myself. An early tutor of mine in radical journalism, the late James Cameron, once confessed that every time he addressed the typewriter he thought to himself: "Today is the day they are going to find me out." (He had been the great chronicler of Indian independence, and when he died was the only man who had seen three nuclear explosions.) I am consoled, when I suffer this very same apprehension, by the thought that the pope and the queen and the president all wake up every morning with a similar gnawing fear. Or that, if they do not, they deserve to be doubted and distrusted even more, if that were possible, than I doubt and distrust them now.

So I have no peroration or clarion note on which to close. Beware the irrational, however seductive. Shun the "transcendent" and all who invite you to subordinate or annihilate yourself. Distrust compassion; prefer dignity for yourself and others. Don't be afraid to be thought arrogant or selfish. Picture all experts as if they were mammals. Never be a spectator of unfairness or stupidity. Seek out argument and disputation for their own sake; the grave will supply plenty of time for silence. Suspect your own motives, and all excuses. Do not live for others any more than you would expect others to live for you.

I shall leave you with a few words from George Konrad, the Hungarian dissident who retained his integrity through some crepuscular times, and who survived his persecutors by writing *Antipolitics* and *The Loser*, and many other lapidary essays and fictions. (When, after the emancipation of his country and society, they came to him and offered him the presidency, he said "No, thanks.") He wrote this in 1987, when the dawn seemed a good way off:

Have a lived life instead of a career. Put yourself in the safekeeping of good taste. Lived freedom will compensate you for a few losses. . . . If you don't like the style of others, cultivate your own. Get to know the tricks of reproduction, be a self-publisher even in conversation, and then the joy of working can fill your days.

May it be so with you, and may you keep your powder dry for the battles ahead, and know when and how to recognise them.